# EASY, DELICIOUS
# DIABETIC RECIPES

Indian-Spiced Monkfish, page 97.

# EASY, DELICIOUS DIABETIC RECIPES

WITH AN INTRODUCTION BY **Robyn Webb, M.S., L.N.**

FOOD PHOTOGRAPHY BY **Renée Comet**

**Oxmoor House**®

# Oxmoor House®

ISBN: 0-8487-2767-3
Printed in the U.S.A.
10 9 8 7 6 5 4 3 2 1

### Easy, Delicious Diabetic Recipes

Director of New Product Development:
**Carolyn M. Clark**
New Product Development Manager: **Lori A. Woehrle**
Senior Editor: **Robert Somerville**
Director of Design: **Kate L. McConnell**
Project Editor: **Ruth Goldberg**
Technical Specialist: **Monika Lynde**
Director of Production: **Carolyn Bounds**
Technical Solutions Specialist: **Richard Hogg**

Design: **Studio A, Alexandria, Virginia**
Photography: **Renée Comet Photography, Inc.**
Food Styling and Recipe Research: **Lisa Cherkasky**
Nutritional Analysis: **Hill Nutrition Associates**

Special Contributors: **Christine Higgins** (project
management); **Leslie Glover Pendleton** (recipe editing);
**Susan Stuck** (research); **Robyn Webb, R.D.** (introduction
and nutrition notes); **Jane Harvey** (copyediting); **Celia
Beattie** (proofreading); **Rose Grant** (index); **Ellen
Calloway** (photo assistance); **Arlene Soodak** (props
coordination). Special thanks to the late **Elizabeth Hiser,
R.D.**, for her nutritional wisdom.

Props: The editors wish to thank the following individuals
and companies: Anthropologie, Kensington, Md.; Bloom-
ingdales, Kensington, Md.; Dansk, Rockville, Md.; French
Country Living, Great Falls, Va.; Charlene Carroll,
Mikasa, Rockville, Md.; Helena Belanger, Simon Pearce,
Bethesda, Md.; Pottery Barn, Chevy Chase, D.C.; Pottery
Barn, Washington, D.C.; Pottery Barn, Kensington, Md.;
Chris Simoncelli, Atlanta, Ga.; Simply Home, Washing-
ton, D.C.; Smith & Hawken, Washington, D.C.; Norma
Cunningham, Sur La Table, McLean, Va.; Karl Utzman,
Teaism, Washington, D.C.; Williams-Sonoma, Kensington,
Md.; Williams-Sonoma, Washington, D.C.

Books produced by Oxmoor House are available at a
special bulk discount for promotional and premium use.
Custom adaptations can also be created to meet your
specific marketing goals.
Call Gary Wright at 1-205-445-6000.

Recipe shown on facing page: Cranberry Poached
Pears, page 159.

Chickpea Salad with Cucumber and Dill Sauce, page 61.

# CONTENTS

# INTRODUCTION

BALANCE

PLANNING

MODERATION

# Good Food for Managing Diabetes—A Balancing Act

**Eating is one of life's great pleasures,** and learning you have diabetes should not keep you from eating well. Every day diabetes researchers are **learning more ways to manage this disease,** and so can you.

**Here's some good news:** Meal planning and cooking for a person with diabetes—yourself or a family member—can be as alive with colors, surprises, and great flavors as it is for anyone else. Gone are the old days of a highly restrictive "diabetic diet." You still need to pay attention to the balance among carbohydrates, proteins, and fats. Portion size is still very important, too, particularly if you've been told you need to lose weight. But that doesn't mean you can't **enjoy delicious and even indulgent meals.** The recipes you'll find in *Easy, Delicious Diabetic Recipes* are proof that rich and creamy textures and **innovative flavors** and ingredients are easy to work into a super-healthy diet.

**A juggling act.** Think of managing diabetes as a learned skill. It takes **practice, focus, and planning.** As with most skills, you need coaches—in this case, a physician and a dietitian. Because diabetes is so serious, you should definitely work with both to **develop an eating and exercise plan that empowers you** to live in maximum health. The suggestions in this book assume that you're involving both your physician and dietitian in setting up a food plan.

**Good nutrition: the cornerstone in treating diabetes.** Guidelines for people with diabetes have changed as medical advances reveal more about treatment of the disease. Years ago a person with diabetes might have received a preprinted, one-size-fits-all "diet" with specific foods and a set calorie level. Today we know that **what's generally healthy for the rest of the population is also healthy for people with diabetes.** Current American Diabetes Association guidelines agree with the "Dietary Guidelines for Americans" issued by the Department of Health and

Human Services and the U.S. Department of Agriculture: Choose a variety of fruits, vegetables, and whole grains; eat a diet low in saturated fat cholesterol and moderate in total fat; choose beverages and foods that help you limit sugar intake; use less salt; and if you drink alcohol, do it moderately.

**Eating well while eating smart.** To feel your best, you need to be vigilant in following nutritional guidelines to maintain control of your blood sugar—the key to managing this disease. If you have been diagnosed with either type 1 or type 2 diabetes, you probably know that the more varied your food plan is, the more easily you will be able to meet all your dietary needs. This book is a collection of delicious recipes that will help you focus on food that will not only keep your diabetes under control but will also satisfy you.

## MAKING SMART FOOD CHOICES

**Reach for fiber-packed vegetables, whole grains, and beans.** Most Americans, whether they have diabetes or not, short-change themselves on fiber—the elements of plant food we can't digest. For people with diabetes, fiber is especially important because it plays a crucial role in maintaining stable blood sugar levels. It is virtually calorie-free; it slows down your eating because it makes you chew longer; it takes up space in your stomach and in your small intestine, where it absorbs water and slows digestion, helping you feel full longer

and keeping your energy level on a more even keel. In addition to fiber, vegetables, whole grains, and beans contain phytochemicals that may help prevent certain cancers and—in the case of oats and many soy products—lower cholesterol, which in turn reduces the chances of heart disease. This is especially important for people with diabetes, who have a greater chance of developing heart disease earlier in life.

**Choose proteins low in saturated fat.** Think small and low fat when selecting proteins. Cut back on meats and dairy products high in saturated fat, which raises blood cholesterol levels and thus your risk of heart disease. Some new research indicates that it may be healthier for people with diabetes to get more of their protein from beans, grains, and soy products.

**Get to know the good fats.** If you have diabetes, the total amount of fat you should eat needs to be determined by your goals for blood glucose control. The best fats are the monounsaturates, found primarily in olive and canola oils. They lower total cholesterol levels without lowering HDL—the "good" cholesterol. Polyunsaturated fats such as corn, cottonseed, and soy oil help lower LDL—the "bad" cholesterol—but they also lower HDL at the same time. Avoid trans-fatty acids, or trans-fats, which are believed to raise overall cholesterol levels. Found in margarine, canned shortening, and most commercial baked goods, trans-fats are created through hydrogenation, a process that essentially makes oil hard at room temperature. Ease up on foods that list "hydrogenated vegetable oil" among the ingredients.

**Cut back on refined starches.** Once a grain has been stripped of its nutrient- and fiber-rich bran and germ, it is known as a refined starch. Refined starches lack digestion-slowing fiber, so they tend to make blood sugar levels soar quickly, then crash. Look for whole-grain products such as brown and wild rice, whole-grain pastas and cereals, and whole-grain breads. The other challenge is to find starches that contain little added fat. There isn't much saturated and overall fat or cholesterol in starches to begin with, but they are often combined with fats in packaged foods. Choose a whole-grain roll over a high-fat croissant, or hearty whole-grain crackers over buttery ones. Because starches raise the level of blood glucose more than fat and protein do, you may need to adjust your activity level or medications if you eat a lot of them.

**Save sweets for treats.** For many years, people with diabetes were told that sweets were strictly off-limits. No longer: Today we know that it is okay to have small portions of sugar and other sweets—with the emphasis on small. Research has shown that carbohydrates like table sugar may not raise the blood sugar any more quickly than carbohydrates such as potatoes, rice, or bread. Unlike foods that also contain fiber and nutrients, however, sugar gives you no nourishment. How the sugar you eat influences your body's blood sugar depends on whether it's part of a fiber-rich meal or eaten alone; how much of it you eat; whether your blood glucose is currently controlled; your weight or cholesterol levels; and how active you are. A major reason to lighten up on sweets is that many, such as cakes and cookies, pack loads of fat that can widen your waistline and clog your arteries. You may need to eat small portions and check your blood sugar one to two hours after eating a sweet. Once you know your own patterns and needs, you can gain confidence in your dessert choices.

**Eat fruit, but watch portion size.** People with diabetes often have concerns about fruit: Will the sugar in fruit cause my blood sugar to rise? Should I avoid fruit juice? Are there fruits I should avoid? How quickly fruit raises the blood sugar level, and how much, depend on your blood sugar level before you eat the fruit; whether you eat it on an empty stomach or after a meal; and how much medication you've taken. Fruit provides fiber, essential minerals like magnesium and potassium, and important disease-fighting antioxidants such as vitamin C and beta carotene, which your body turns into vitamin A. Pay careful attention to portion sizes. In general, a serving of fruit is considered one small to medium-size piece of fruit, ½ cup fruit or juice, or ¼ cup dried fruit.

**Lighten up on salt.** The recommendation for sodium is about 2,400 milligrams a day—less if you have high blood pressure. Most Americans consume twice that amount. The easiest way to ditch some sodium is to rely less on packaged convenience foods, which are loaded with salt. To enhance flavors when cooking, replace salt with fresh herbs, spices, and lemon.

**Drink in moderation.** If you choose to drink alcohol, talk to a dietitian about how to work it into your food plan. Generally, you should go easy, drink only with meals, and only when your blood sugar is under control. If you are not on medications and are not overweight, a portion of alcohol can substitute for a fat in your food plan. Alcohol may also be used in cooking to add flavor while helping to reduce the fat in a recipe.

## MAINTAINING GOOD CONTROL

**Size does matter.** Although people with diabetes can choose from a wide array of foods, portion size still matters. It may seem unlikely that just a scoop of mashed potatoes or one more teaspoon of oil can make a difference, but it does—to both body weight and blood sugar control. If you have diabetes, weight control is especially important. Extra calories make it more difficult to lose or maintain weight, or manage

blood sugar levels. Until you can really eyeball serving sizes correctly, you'd be smart to rely on such tools as measuring spoons and cups and a food scale.

**The exchange principle.** For many years the food exchange system has been used as a meal planning approach for people with diabetes. Exchange lists are foods grouped so that each serving has about the same amount of carbohydrate, protein, fat, and calories as the other foods on that list. Any food on a list can be "exchanged" or traded for any other on the same list.

The lists are organized into three groups:

- **The carbohydrate group** includes starches like bread or cereal, fruit, milk, vegetables, and any other carbohydrates.

- **The meat and meat substitute group** is divided into very lean, lean, medium-fat, and high-fat foods.

- **The fat group** includes monounsaturated, polyunsaturated, and saturated fats.

Foods are listed with their serving sizes, measured after cooking. The advantage of the exchange system is that it allows flexibility in planning meals. For instance, you can trade a slice of bread for ½ cup cooked cereal or one small waffle, as all have the same number of calories and carbohydrate grams.

To use this system, you need an individualized food program. Once you and a dietitian have worked out a plan that also accounts for your medication or insulin and exercise level, the food exchange system can provide an overall well-balanced food plan.

**The glycemic index.** Since carbohydrates have the greatest impact on blood sugar, paying attention to the choice of carbohydrates may be helpful. Researchers have developed an index that ranks foods according to how quickly and how much they raise blood sugar levels in comparison with pure sugar. That comparison is given a number: For example, pure sugar has a rating of 100; a plain baked potato, 87; orange juice, 49; and yogurt, 38. A high number indicates a rapid "spike" in blood sugar level, followed by a rapid drop, while a low number indicates a slower, steadier rise and fall in blood sugar. The theory behind the glycemic index is that "slow" carbs are usually better choices than "fast" carbs. Research suggests that foods with a low glycemic index can have good effects on blood sugar, cholesterol, and triglyceride levels and may reduce the risk of kidney disease.

But the index should not be used in place of the food exchange system or the food pyramid guidelines. You need to consider lots of things when choosing carbohydrate foods: the type of carbohydrate, how it is going to be cooked, fiber content, the protein and fat in the meal, and pre-meal blood glucose levels.

**FILL UP ON FIBER**

*Fiber—elements of plant food that we can't digest—is virtually calorie-free and slows down your eating because it makes you chew longer, holds many times its weight in water, and fills you up. Dietary fiber is either soluble or insoluble. Oats, whole-grain rye, and beans are the richest sources of soluble fiber, which helps lower blood cholesterol and slows the digestion of carbohydrates. Insoluble fiber—the type that predominates in whole wheat and other grains—may also play a role in preventing disease.*

For example, adding butter to a baked potato and serving it as part of a meal with meat and a salad improves the effect of the potato on blood sugar, since the fat, protein, and fiber in the other foods will offset the high index of the potato. Consult a registered dietitian to develop a food program tailored to your needs.

## LIVING SUCCESSFULLY WITH DIABETES

**Choose a plan and stick with it.** Research suggests that for people with diabetes, having a diet plan and staying on it is more important than which plan you choose—high carb/high fiber, low fat, or weight loss. A registered dietitian can help you decide the best plan for you and determine the number of servings from each food group you will need for your meals and snacks. Other factors to consider when planning your meals: your diabetes medication schedule, how often you tend to experience low blood sugar, your desire for snacks, whether you eat out often, desire for weight loss, and activity levels. But the message is clear: Eat at least three well-balanced meals that each include carbohydrate, fat, and protein, and use snacks as needed to prevent low blood sugar.

*Robyn Webb, M.S., L.N.*
Associate Editor, *Diabetes Forecast Magazine*

**How to use our nutritional analyses:** The numbers that accompany each recipe represent the nutrients found in a single serving of the finished product. Keep in mind that 1 gram of protein = 4 calories; 1 gram of fat = 9 calories; and 1 gram of carbohydrate = 4 calories. You can determine your daily requirements of nutritional elements from the following information.

**Calories:** To maintain your current weight, you need roughly 12 to 15 calories per pound of body weight each day, depending on your level of activity. For example, if you weigh 135 pounds and are quite active, multiply 135 x 15 calories for a total of 2,025 calories per day.

**Fat:** Whether you have diabetes or not, experts say no more than 30 percent of calories should come from fat. To estimate how many grams of fat to aim for, multiply your daily caloric level by 30 percent—that is, by .3—and then divide by 9. For example, if you need 2,000 calories per day: 2,000 calories x .3 = 600 calories / 9 calories per gram of fat = 67 grams.

**Saturated Fat:** Of your total daily calories, only about 10 percent should come from saturated fat. That works out to about 22 grams of saturated fat per day in the example above. But keep in mind that for the best protection, you want to cut saturated fat as much as possible.

**Carbohydrates:** A gram of carbohydrate contains 4 calories. About 50 to 60 percent of your daily calories should come from carbohydrates, which translates to 250 to 300 grams in our example of a 2,000-calorie diet. If you have high triglyceride levels, it's smarter to aim for the lower end of the carbohydrate range.

**Protein:** Adults need about .4 gram of protein per pound of body weight a day to stay healthy, or about 54 grams per day for a 135-pound person. Ideally, as much of that as possible should come from plant sources, such as beans, soy products, and other legumes, which are low in saturated fat. Eating too much protein causes your kidneys to work overtime to get rid of protein waste products.

**Cholesterol:** The recommended limit is 300 milligrams of dietary cholesterol per day. But keep in mind that dietary cholesterol levels don't translate directly to blood cholesterol levels. Saturated fat raises blood cholesterol levels more than dietary cholesterol does.

**Sodium:** The current recommended limit is 2,400 milligrams of sodium a day, roughly the amount in a teaspoon of salt. If you're prone to high blood pressure, you should consume even less sodium.

**Fiber:** Health experts recommend eating at least 25 to 35 grams of dietary fiber a day. That's a lot; most of us get less than half as much. Breakfast is a great fiber opportunity—whole-grain or bran cereals and fruit are excellent sources. And if you find you need a snack during the day, use it as a chance to meet your fiber quota by eating fruits, vegetables, and whole grains.

# HEALTHY
## STARTS

**SERVES: 4**

1 ripe papaya (about 1 lb.), peeled, seeded, and cut into chunks

2 tsp. fresh lemon juice

¼ tsp. ground allspice

¾ cup fresh orange juice

2 tsp. honey

1 cup buttermilk

4 ice cubes

Lemon slices for garnish

**CHILLED PAPAYA SHAKE**

1 Puree the papaya, lemon juice, ⅛ teaspoon of the allspice, and about half of the orange juice in a blender or a food processor. Add the honey, buttermilk, the remaining orange juice and the ice cubes, and blend the mixture until it is smooth—about 30 seconds in a blender or 1 minute in a food processor.

2 Pour the papaya shake into glasses, sprinkle with some of the remaining allspice, and garnish with a slice of lemon.

**HEALTH NOTE** | *Papayas are rich in beta carotene, an important antioxidant that may play a role in the prevention of certain cancers.*

**SERVES: 2**

1 large banana, peeled and sliced

1 ripe peach, peeled, halved, pitted, and sliced, or 1 cup frozen unsweetened sliced peaches

1 cup buttermilk

¼ cup fresh orange juice

2 strawberries for garnish (optional)

**BANANA-PEACH BUTTERMILK SHAKE**

1 Wrap the banana slices in plastic wrap and freeze them for at least 6 hours. If you are using fresh peach slices, wrap and freeze them at the same time.

2 When you are ready to prepare the shake, put the banana and peach slices, the buttermilk, and orange juice into a food processor or a blender; process the mixture until smooth—about 1 minute. Pour the puree into tall glasses, and garnish each glass with a strawberry, if desired. Serve the shakes immediately.

**CHILLED PAPAYA SHAKE:** DIABETIC EXCHANGE: **1** FRUIT   ¼ SKIM MILK

CALORIES: **87**   FAT: **.7 G**   SAT. FAT: **.4 G**   CARBOHYDRATES: **18 G**   PROTEIN: **3 G**   CHOLESTEROL: **2 MG**   SODIUM: **67 MG**   FIBER: **.8 G**

**BANANA-PEACH BUTTERMILK SHAKE:** DIABETIC EXCHANGE: **1¾** FRUIT   ½ SKIM MILK

CALORIES: **151**   FAT: **1 G**   SAT. FAT: **.8 G**   CARBOHYDRATES: **32 G**   PROTEIN: **5 G**   CHOLESTEROL: **5 MG**   SODIUM: **130 MG**   FIBER: **2 G**

# Zucchini-Raisin Muffins

**MAKES 12 MUFFINS**

1½ cups buttermilk

1 cup rolled oats

½ cup ready-to-eat whole-bran cereal (NOTE: "buds" such as All-Bran™—not flakes)

2 tbsp. butter

2 tbsp. light brown sugar

1 egg, lightly beaten

1 cup whole-wheat flour

1 tsp. baking powder

1 tsp. baking soda

¼ tsp. salt

¼ tsp. ground cinnamon

1 cup coarsely grated zucchini, squeezed dry

½ cup dark raisins

¼ cup coarsely chopped walnuts

1 Preheat the oven to 400°.

2 Spray 12 muffin tin cups with cooking spray or line them with paper liners.

3 Combine the buttermilk, oats, and cereal in a medium bowl; set aside for 30 minutes.

4 Cream together the butter and brown sugar in another medium bowl, using an electric mixer. Beat in the egg. Stir in the flour, baking powder, baking soda, salt, and cinnamon.

5 Add the flour mixture to the oats mixture and stir to combine. Stir in the zucchini, raisins, and walnuts.

6 Divide the batter among the muffin cups and bake for 35 minutes, or until a toothpick inserted into a muffin comes out clean.

**HEALTH NOTE** | *Most muffins are very low in fiber and crammed with white flour, sugar, and fat. This recipe packs whole grains, vegetables, fruits, and nuts into a tasty morning treat with a respectable 3 grams of fiber. Starting with one of these muffins is a good way to begin to get the 25 grams of fiber you need each day.*

DIABETIC EXCHANGE: **1½ STARCH   1 FAT**

CALORIES: **148**   FAT: **5 G**   SAT. FAT: **2 G**   CARBOHYDRATES: **23 G**   PROTEIN: **5 G**   CHOLESTEROL: **24 MG**   SODIUM: **277 MG**   FIBER: **3 G**

# Buttermilk Banana **Bread**

1 Preheat the oven to 350°.

2 Spray a 9-by-5-inch loaf pan with cooking spray.

3 Combine the flour, baking soda, and salt in a small bowl.

4 Beat together the egg, honey, and oil until smooth in a large bowl, using an electric mixer. Add half of the flour mixture and beat until smooth. Beat in the buttermilk, then add the remaining flour mixture, blending well after each addition. Add the mashed banana and blend well. Add the currants and walnuts, and stir until combined.

5 Pour the batter into the pan and bake for 50 minutes, or until a toothpick inserted into the loaf comes out almost dry. Turn the bread out onto a rack to cool completely before slicing.

**SERVES: 16**

1¼ cups unbleached all-purpose flour

½ tsp. baking soda

¼ tsp. salt

1 large egg

⅓ cup honey

2 tbsp. canola oil

¼ cup buttermilk

1 cup mashed ripe banana

¼ cup currants or raisins

¼ cup chopped walnuts

**EDITOR'S NOTE** | *Who can pass up a warm slice of banana bread? Most of the sweetness is derived from the potassium-rich bananas and the nutrient-packed dried fruit. And with only 2 tablespoons of oil, this bread is low in fat but not short on taste.*

DIABETIC EXCHANGE: ¾ STARCH    ½ CARBOHYDRATE    ½ FAT

CALORIES: **110**    FAT: **3 G**    SAT. FAT: **.4 G**    CARBOHYDRATES: **19 G**    PROTEIN: **2 G**    CHOLESTEROL: **13 MG**    SODIUM: **84 MG**    FIBER: **.7 G**

HONEY

OATS

BLUEBERRIES

# Blueberry Oat Bran Muffins

1 Preheat the oven to 375°.

2 Spray 12 muffin tin cups with cooking spray or line them with
paper liners.

3 Combine the buttermilk, honey, oil, and egg whites in a small bowl.

4 Combine the oats, oat bran, flour, baking powder, and salt in a large bowl
and make a well in the center. Add the milk mixture and the blueberries,
and stir just until combined; do not overmix.

5 Divide the batter among the muffin cups and bake for 25 minutes,
or until a toothpick inserted into a muffin comes out clean.

**HEALTH NOTE** | *Oats have been proven to improve cholesterol levels and may
play a role in the prevention of heart disease, a principal health issue faced by
many people with diabetes. In addition, blueberries are one of the best fruit
sources of disease-fighting antioxidants.*

**MAKES 12 MUFFINS**

1 cup buttermilk

¼ cup honey

2 tbsp. canola oil

2 egg whites, lightly beaten

1 cup rolled oats

1 cup oat bran

½ cup unbleached all-purpose flour

2 tsp. baking powder

Pinch of salt

1½ cups fresh or unsweetened
frozen blueberries, thawed

DIABETIC EXCHANGE: 1⅓ STARCH    ½ FAT

CALORIES: **129**    FAT: **4 G**    SAT. FAT: **.4 G**    CARBOHYDRATES: **23 G**    PROTEIN: **4 G**    CHOLESTEROL: **.8 MG**    SODIUM: **126 MG**    FIBER: **2 G**

**FRESH YOGURT CHEESE**

1  Line a large sieve with a double layer of cheesecloth or a large, round paper coffee filter. Place the lined sieve over a deep bowl so that the yogurt can effectively drain, and spoon the yogurt into the sieve. Cover the bowl and sieve with plastic wrap, refrigerate, and let the yogurt drain overnight.

2  Discard the whey that has collected in the bowl and transfer the yogurt cheese to another bowl—the cheese should be very thick. Yogurt cheese will keep, covered in the refrigerator, for 2 weeks.

**TIP** | *Make yogurt cheese a staple in your household. A tasty, healthful substitute for cream cheese, this smooth, slightly tangy spread can be used as a basis for sweet or savory spreads, for dips, and in baking. Yogurt is one of the best sources of calcium, necessary for developing and keeping strong bones.*

**SMOKED SALMON SPREAD**

1  Combine the yogurt cheese, chives, salmon, pepper, paprika, lemon juice, and salt in a medium bowl. Refrigerate the spread for at least 2 hours before serving it so that the flavors can meld.

---

**SERVES: 6**

3 cups plain low-fat yogurt

---

**SERVES: 6**

1½ cups yogurt cheese
  (recipe above)

3 tbsp. finely chopped fresh chives
  or scallions

1½ oz. smoked salmon, minced

¼ tsp. white pepper

⅛ tsp. sweet paprika,
  preferably Hungarian

1 tsp. fresh lemon juice

⅛ tsp. salt

---

**FRESH YOGURT CHEESE:** DIABETIC EXCHANGE: ½ SKIM MILK  ¼ FAT

CALORIES: 50     FAT: 1 G     SAT. FAT: 0 G     CARBOHYDRATES: 2 G     PROTEIN: 5 G     CHOLESTEROL: 3 MG     SODIUM: 36 MG     FIBER: 0 G

**SMOKED SALMON SPREAD:** DIABETIC EXCHANGE: ½ SKIM MILK  ¼ FAT  ¼ VERY LEAN MEAT

CALORIES: 59     FAT: 2 G     SAT. FAT: .1 G     CARBOHYDRATES: 3 G     PROTEIN: 7 G     CHOLESTEROL: 4 MG     SODIUM: 227 MG     FIBER: 0 G

# Whole-Wheat Biscuits with Bulgur and Citrus

**MAKES 16 BISCUITS**

¼ cup bulgur

⅓ cup boiling water

1 cup plain low-fat yogurt

2 tsp. grated orange zest

1 tsp. grated lemon zest

2 tbsp. canola oil

1½ cups whole-wheat flour

3 tbsp. sugar

1½ tsp. baking powder

⅛ tsp. salt

**HEALTH NOTE** *Bulgur wheat, a grain rich in fiber, makes these much more nutritious than most morning biscuits. Foods that are high in fiber help keep blood sugar levels stable.*

1 Put the bulgur into a large bowl and pour in boiling water. Let the bulgur stand, covered, until it is tender—about 15 minutes.

2 Preheat the oven to 375°. Lightly oil a baking sheet or line it with parchment paper.

3 Drain the bulgur thoroughly, and return it to the bowl. Stir in the yogurt, orange zest, lemon zest and oil. Sift the flour, sugar, baking powder, and salt over the bulgur mixture and stir them together just until they are combined. The dough will be quite sticky.

4 Turn the dough out onto a heavily floured surface. Dust your hands and the top of the dough with flour. Flatten the dough with your hands until it is about ¼ inch thick, using flour as needed to keep the dough from sticking.

5 Using a 2½-inch cookie cutter, cut out as many biscuits as possible and put them on the baking sheet. Press the scraps of dough together and use them to make more biscuits.

6 Bake the biscuits until they are lightly browned—15 to 20 minutes. Serve the biscuits hot.

DIABETIC EXCHANGE: ¾ STARCH    ½ FAT

CALORIES: 82    FAT: 2 G    SAT. FAT: .3 G    CARBOHYDRATES: 13 G    PROTEIN: 3 G    CHOLESTEROL: .9 MG    SODIUM: 75 MG    FIBER: 2 G

TOMATO

OREGANO

ZUCCHINI

# Spanish Omelet

1 Heat 1½ tablespoons of the oil in a heavy frying pan over medium heat. Add the onion and cook until soft, about 3 minutes. Add the garlic and zucchini, cover, and cook the vegetables gently for 10 minutes, stirring occasionally. Remove from the heat.

2 Boil the potato in a small saucepan until tender, 25 to 30 minutes. Remove. Add the beans to the boiling water and cook until tender, about 5 minutes. Coarsely chop the potato, and cut the beans into 1-inch lengths.

3 Beat together the eggs and egg whites, salt, and some black pepper in a large bowl. Gently stir in the cooked vegetables, tomato, and oregano.

4 Heat the remaining oil in a 10-inch nonstick ovenproof skillet and pour in the egg mixture. Cook the omelet gently over medium heat for 3 to 4 minutes, or until the underside is pale gold.

5 Place the pan under a preheated broiler and cook the omelet for 2 to 3 minutes more, or until it is just set. Cut it into quarters and serve.

**SERVES: 4**

2 tbsp. olive oil

1 onion, chopped

2 cloves garlic, chopped

2 small zucchini (about 4 oz.), trimmed and thinly sliced

1 large potato (about 8 oz.), peeled

4 oz. fresh green beans, trimmed

2 eggs

2 egg whites

½ tsp. salt

Freshly ground black pepper

1 large fresh tomato (about 5 oz.), peeled, seeded, and chopped

½ tbsp. chopped fresh oregano, or ½ tsp. dried oregano

**EDITOR'S NOTE** | *Wake up your taste buds with the enticing aroma of fresh-cooked eggs laced with onions, garlic, and garden-fresh vegetables. Eliminating 2 egg yolks cuts the fat found in a typical omelet.*

DIABETIC EXCHANGE: ½ STARCH   2 VEGETABLE   1½ FAT   ½ LEAN MEAT

CALORIES: **186**   FAT: **10 G**   SAT. FAT: **2 G**   CARBOHYDRATES: **19 G**   PROTEIN: **8 G**   CHOLESTEROL: **106 MG**   SODIUM: **359 MG**   FIBER: **3 G**

# SOUPS

1 Combine the tomatoes and their liquid, cucumber, scallions, bell pepper, basil, vinegar, Worcestershire, garlic, black pepper, and salt in a large bowl. Stir well to break up the tomatoes. Cover the bowl and refrigerate the gazpacho 4 hours, or until thoroughly chilled.

2 Stir the soup to reblend it before serving.

**HEALTH NOTE** | *Gazpacho is an easy way to incorporate vegetables into your meals: A single helping takes care of two of the three to five daily servings of vegetables you need.*

**SERVES: 4**

1 can (28 oz.) diced tomatoes, with their liquid, or 6 very ripe, medium tomatoes, diced

1½ cups finely chopped unpeeled cucumber

½ cup finely chopped scallions

⅓ cup finely diced red or yellow bell pepper

¼ cup chopped fresh basil, or 1 tbsp. plus 1 tsp. dried basil

2 tbsp. red wine vinegar

1 tsp. Worcestershire sauce

1 small clove garlic, minced

½ tsp. freshly ground black pepper

Pinch of salt

DIABETIC EXCHANGE: **2 VEGETABLE**

CALORIES:**56**    FAT:**.6 G**    SAT. FAT:**.1 G**    CARBOHYDRATES:**12 G**    PROTEIN:**3 G**    CHOLESTEROL:**0 MG**    SODIUM:**375 MG**    FIBER:**3 G**

### TOASTED CORN SOUP
**SERVES: 4**

4 medium ears of corn, or
4 cups frozen corn kernels

4 cups fat-free, reduced-sodium chicken broth

1 large carrot, peeled and chopped

1 medium onion, chopped

2 cloves garlic, pressed or minced

Basil Salsa (recipe follows)

Fresh basil sprigs for garnish

Salt to taste

### BASIL SALSA
**MAKES SIX ¼-CUP PORTIONS**

1 large ripe tomato, diced

¼ cup chopped fresh basil leaves

2 tbsp. fresh lime juice

1 tbsp. minced, seeded fresh jalapeño chili

**TOASTED CORN SOUP**

1 Remove and discard the corn husks and silks; rinse ears.

2 Place a 10- to 12-inch frying pan over medium-high heat. When pan is hot, add ears of corn and toast, turning as needed, until kernels are lightly browned, about 10 minutes. Remove the corn from the pan and let it cool. (Follow the same procedure for frozen corn kernels.)

3 Combine the broth, carrot, onion, and garlic in a 3- to 4-quart pan, and bring to a boil. Simmer until the vegetables are tender, about 10 minutes.

4 Meanwhile, cut the kernels off cobs with a sharp knife and add to broth mixture. Simmer, covered, for 5 minutes.

5 In batches, puree the soup in a blender until smooth. Rub the soup through a fine sieve set over a bowl; discard the solids. Serve the soup hot or chilled, in bowls, topped with some basil salsa and basil sprigs.

**BASIL SALSA**

1 Combine the tomato, basil, lime juice, and jalapeño in a bowl. The salsa can be made 1 day in advance, kept covered and refrigerated.

**TOASTED CORN SOUP:** DIABETIC EXCHANGE: **2** STARCH **1** VEGETABLE

CALORIES:**177** FAT:**2 G** SAT. FAT:**.3 G** CARBOHYDRATES:**37 G** PROTEIN:**9 G** CHOLESTEROL:**0 MG** SODIUM:**654 MG** FIBER:**6 G**

**BASIL SALSA:** DIABETIC EXCHANGE: ½ VEGETABLE

CALORIES:**11** FAT:**.1 G** SAT. FAT:**0 G** CARBOHYDRATES:**3 G** PROTEIN:**5 G** CHOLESTEROL:**0 MG** SODIUM:**4 MG** FIBER:**.6 G**

LIME

JALAPEÑO

BASIL

1  Combine the tomatoes, ½ cup of rice, celery, onion, basil, tomato paste, garlic, salt, pepper, bay leaf, and 1 quart of water in a large saucepan. Bring the mixture to a boil, reduce the heat, and simmer, covered, about 30 minutes, stirring occasionally and breaking up the tomatoes with the edge of the spoon.

2  Let the soup cool about 30 minutes; remove and discard the bay leaf.

3  In batches, puree the soup in a food processor or a blender.

4  Return the soup to the saucepan, stir in the remaining rice, and reheat over a medium heat.

**EDITOR'S NOTE** | *This light soup can be made with ingredients you probably have on hand.*

**SERVES: 6**

2 lb. fresh, ripe tomatoes, cored and quartered, or 1 can (28 oz.) tomatoes, with their liquid

1½ cups cooked rice

1 cup chopped celery

½ cup chopped onion

¼ cup chopped fresh basil, or 1 tbsp. dried basil

3 tbsp. tomato paste

2 cloves garlic, chopped

Pinch of salt

¼ tsp. freshly ground black pepper

1 bay leaf

DIABETIC EXCHANGE: ¾ STARCH   2 VEGETABLE

CALORIES: 99   FAT: .7 G   SAT. FAT: .1 G   CARBOHYDRATES: 22 G   PROTEIN: 3 G   CHOLESTEROL: 0 MG   SODIUM: 119 MG   FIBER: 3 G

**SERVES: 4**

2 cups fat-free, reduced-sodium chicken broth

¼ cup dry sherry or dry white wine

2 cloves garlic, minced

1½ tsp. paprika

⅛ tsp. crumbled saffron threads, or ¼ tsp. turmeric

½ tsp. salt

¼ tsp. freshly ground black pepper

½ cup long-grain white rice

¾ lb. skinless, boneless chicken breasts, cut into 1-inch cubes

1 green bell pepper, cut into 1-inch squares

1 red bell pepper, cut into 1-inch squares

1 cup frozen peas

1 Combine the broth, 3 cups of water, sherry, garlic, paprika, saffron, salt, and black pepper in a flameproof casserole. Bring the mixture to a boil, add the rice, and simmer for 5 minutes to blend the flavors.

2 Add the chicken and bell peppers to the pan and simmer, covered, until the rice is tender and the chicken is cooked through, about 15 minutes.

3 Stir in the peas and simmer until the peas are heated through, about 1 minute.

**TIP** *The finest and most expensive saffron comes in packets of individual threads, which should be gently crumbled just before using and then measured with a measuring spoon. Measure the less expensive powdered saffron as you would any other spice. Paprika comes in both mild imported and U.S.-grown varieties and in hot Hungarian. The recipes in this book use mild paprika.*

DIABETIC EXCHANGE: **1½** STARCH   **1** VEGETABLE   **2¾** VERY LEAN MEAT

CALORIES: **247**   FAT: **2 G**   SAT. FAT: **.4 G**   CARBOHYDRATES: **28 G**   PROTEIN: **25 G**   CHOLESTEROL: **49 MG**   SODIUM: **699 MG**   FIBER: **2 G**

WHITE WINE

SAFFRON

BELL PEPPERS

SOY SAUCE

TOFU

SNOW PEAS

# Asian Chicken Soup

1  Combine the broth, 1½ cups of water, chicken, and garlic in a medium saucepan and bring to a boil. Reduce to a simmer, cover, and cook until the chicken is cooked through, about 10 minutes. With a slotted spoon, transfer the chicken to a cutting board and dice.

2  Add the bell peppers, vinegar, soy sauce, and ginger and simmer for 2 minutes. Stir in the cabbage, capellini, snow peas, scallions, diced chicken, and more water to cover, if necessary. Boil until the capellini is tender, about 2 minutes more.

3  Stir in the tofu and sesame oil, ladle the soup into 4 bowls, and serve.

---

**EDITOR'S NOTE** | *This intriguing noodle soup is a wonderful showcase for the contrasting textures and tastes characteristic of Asian cooking.*

**SERVES: 4**

4 cups fat-free, reduced-sodium chicken broth

1¼ lb. skinless, boneless chicken breasts

2 cloves garlic, minced

2 red bell peppers, diced

3 tbsp. cider vinegar

1 tbsp. reduced-sodium soy sauce

¾ tsp. ground ginger

3 cups, ½-inch-wide shredded cabbage

3 oz. capellini noodles, broken into small pieces

¼ lb. snow peas, cut into ½-inch diagonal pieces

2 scallions, finely chopped

¼ lb. drained firm tofu, cut into ½-inch chunks

¼ tsp. sesame oil

DIABETIC EXCHANGE: **1 STARCH**  **2½ VEGETABLE**  **½ FAT**  **5 VERY LEAN MEAT**

CALORIES:**338**  FAT:**5 G**  SAT. FAT:**1 G**  CARBOHYDRATES:**28 G**  PROTEIN:**45 G**  CHOLESTEROL:**82 MG**  SODIUM:**878 MG**  FIBER:**3 G**

**SERVES: 6**

1 winter squash (about 2½ lb.) such as butternut or acorn

1 can (12 oz.) spicy vegetable juice

1 cup chopped green bell pepper

1 cup fresh or frozen corn kernels

1 tbsp. chopped fresh basil, or 1 tsp. dried basil

Pinch of salt

1  Preheat the oven to 400°.

2  Line a baking pan with foil.

3  Halve the squash and remove the seeds. Place the squash cut sides down in the pan and bake for 40 minutes, or until the squash is tender when pierced with a knife. Set aside to cool for about 15 minutes.

4  Scoop the squash into a large saucepan and mash it with a potato masher or fork to remove any large lumps, or puree in a food processor or blender. Add 1½ cups of water, the vegetable juice, bell pepper, corn, basil, and salt, and bring to a boil. Reduce the heat and simmer for 10 minutes. Serve the soup hot or chilled.

**HEALTH NOTE** *All kinds of winter squash are very high in beta carotene and potassium and are a good source of iron. If you prefer, you may simplify this recipe by substituting a 15-ounce can of pumpkin puree for the squash.*

DIABETIC EXCHANGE: **1¼ STARCH** **½ VEGETABLE**

CALORIES: **111**   FAT: **.5 G**   SAT. FAT: **.1 G**   CARBOHYDRATES: **27 G**   PROTEIN: **3 G**   CHOLESTEROL: **0 MG**   SODIUM: **219 MG**   FIBER: **4 G**

**SERVES: 8**

1½ cups fat-free, reduced-sodium
  chicken or vegetable broth

1 large russet or other baking potato
  (about ¾ lb.), peeled and diced

1½ tbsp. unsalted butter

1 tbsp. canola oil

1 red onion, coarsely chopped

2 small leeks, trimmed, cleaned,
  and thinly sliced

4 scallions, trimmed and thinly sliced

1 large carrot, peeled and diced

2½ lb. Swiss chard, washed,
  the stems cut into ½-inch pieces,
  the leaves coarsely chopped

¼ tsp. salt

Juice of ½ lemon

Freshly ground black pepper

1 tbsp. finely chopped parsley
  for garnish (optional)

1  Combine the broth and the potato cubes in a small saucepan and simmer, covered, until the potatoes are very tender, about 10 minutes. Drain the potatoes, reserving the broth, and puree with a food mill or press through a fine-meshed sieve. (Potatoes pureed in a food processor or a blender become gluey.) Stir the broth into the potato puree and set aside.

2  In a large pot, heat the butter and oil over medium heat. Add the onion, leeks, and scallions and cook, covered, stirring occasionally, until soft, about 5 minutes.

3  Add ½ inch of water and the carrots and simmer for 5 minutes. Add the chard stems and cook them, covered, until they are tender—3 to 5 minutes. Add the chard leaves and cook, stirring occasionally, for 10 minutes.

4  Stir the potato puree into the pot and cook until the stew is heated through. Stir in the salt, lemon juice, and black pepper. Garnish with the parsley, if using, and serve at once.

**HEALTH NOTE** | *In addition to providing lots of fiber, Swiss chard is very high in beta carotene. The red onion, leeks, and scallions give this stew many layers of both sweet and savory flavors.*

DIABETIC EXCHANGE: ½ STARCH  2 VEGETABLE  ¾ FAT

CALORIES: **117**   FAT: **4 G**   SAT. FAT: **1.5 G**   CARBOHYDRATES: **18 G**   PROTEIN: **4 G**   CHOLESTEROL: **6 MG**   SODIUM: **480 MG**   FIBER: **4 G**

1   In a large pot, cook the onion and minced garlic in the oil over medium heat, stirring frequently, until the onion has softened, about 5 minutes. Stir in the carrots and sweet potatoes and cook until they are softened, about 5 minutes.

2   Stir in the tomato, split peas, 5 cups of water, thyme, salt, and pepper. Bring to a boil, reduce to a simmer, and cover. Simmer, stirring occasionally, until the split peas are tender, about 35 minutes.

3   Meanwhile, preheat the oven to 400°. Rub both sides of the bread with the cut sides of the halved garlic; discard the garlic. Cut the bread into 1-inch pieces for croutons, place on a baking sheet, and bake for 5 minutes, or until pale golden; set aside.

4   Transfer the pea mixture to a food processor and puree until smooth. Return the puree to the pot, stir in the turkey and lemon juice, and cook, uncovered, just until the turkey is heated through. Ladle the soup into 4 bowls and sprinkle the croutons on top.

**EDITOR'S NOTE** | *Between them, the sweet potatoes and split peas make this soup a great source of fiber and beta carotene; they also give it a pleasing color.*

**SERVES: 4**

1 large onion, finely chopped

4 cloves garlic, minced, plus 2 cloves garlic, halved

1 tbsp. olive oil

2 carrots, thinly sliced

¾ lb. sweet potatoes, peeled and thinly sliced

1 cup fresh or canned chopped tomato

1 cup green split peas, picked over and rinsed

¾ tsp. dried thyme

¼ tsp. salt

¼ tsp. freshly ground black pepper

4 slices (1 oz. each) crusty Italian bread

6 oz. smoked turkey, cut into ½-inch dice

1 tbsp. fresh lemon juice

DIABETIC EXCHANGE: 4 STARCH    2½ VEGETABLE    ¾ FAT    1¼ VERY LEAN MEAT

CALORIES: 442    FAT: 7 G    SAT. FAT: 1 G    CARBOHYDRATES: 72 G    PROTEIN: 26 G    CHOLESTEROL: 22 MG    SODIUM: 774 MG    FIBER: 8 G

RED BELL PEPPER

BACON

SAGE

1 Cook the bacon in a medium saucepan over medium-low heat until crisp. Pour off all but 1 tablespoon of fat.

2 Add the bell pepper, carrots, onions, and garlic to the saucepan and cook, covered, until the vegetables are softened, about 7 minutes.

3 Add the flour and cook, stirring, 1 minute. Add 1 cup of water, the milk, bay leaf, salt, white pepper, and sage and simmer until the soup is slightly thickened, about 4 minutes. Add the beans and simmer for 10 minutes.

4 Stir in the corn and cook just until heated through. Discard the bay leaf.

**HEALTH NOTE** | *Beans are a superb source of fiber, providing 3 to 10 grams per cup, depending on the type, and make a great, nearly fat-free stand-in for animal protein. The bit of bacon in this soup adds flavor but little overall fat.*

---

**SERVES: 4**

2 strips of bacon, diced

¾ cup diced red bell pepper

½ cup chopped carrots

½ cup diced onions

2 cloves garlic, minced

1½ tbsp. unbleached, all-purpose flour

1 cup skim milk

1 bay leaf

½ tsp. salt

¼ tsp. white pepper

¼ tsp. dried sage

1½ cups canned white beans, rinsed and drained

1 cup frozen or drained canned corn kernels

---

DIABETIC EXCHANGE: 1¼ STARCH   1¾ VEGETABLE   ¼ SKIM MILK   1 FAT

CALORIES: 198   FAT: 5 G   SAT. FAT: 2 G   CARBOHYDRATES: 30 G   PROTEIN: 10 G   CHOLESTEROL: 6 MG   SODIUM: 590 MG   FIBER: 5 G

**SERVES: 4**

1 tsp. olive oil

2 cups coarsely diced green bell pepper

1 large onion, coarsely chopped

1 cup diced celery

½ cup diced Canadian bacon

2 cloves garlic, minced

⅓ cup dried lentils

2 medium tomatoes, cut into 1-inch cubes

1 cup elbow macaroni

½ tsp. salt

2 tsp. chopped fresh oregano

¼ tsp. black pepper

¼ cup grated Parmesan cheese

1 Heat the oil in a large, heavy-bottomed saucepan over medium heat. Add the bell pepper, onion, celery, Canadian bacon, and garlic, and cook, stirring, until the vegetables are softened, about 5 minutes. Stir in the lentils, tomatoes, and 2 quarts of water; cover the pan and bring to a boil. Reduce the heat and simmer for 20 minutes. Add the macaroni and simmer for 10 minutes more.

2 Add the salt, oregano, and black pepper. Sprinkle with the Parmesan before serving.

---

**HEALTH NOTE** | *There are as many versions of minestrone as there are cooks; this one uses protein-rich lentils, which provide much of the fiber in this dish—5 grams per serving.*

DIABETIC EXCHANGE: **2** STARCH    **2** VEGETABLE    ¼ FAT    ¾ LEAN MEAT

CALORIES: **267**    FAT: **5 G**    SAT. FAT: **2 G**    CARBOHYDRATES: **42 G**    PROTEIN: **15 G**    CHOLESTEROL: **13 MG**    SODIUM: **671 MG**    FIBER: **5 G**

PARMESAN

OREGANO

LENTILS

1 Squeeze the sausages out of their casings and brown the meat, breaking it up, in the oil in a large saucepan over a medium heat. Sprinkle the flour on top and cook, stirring, for 2 minutes.

2 Add the tomatoes and their liquid, the onion, bell pepper, celery, thyme, bay leaf, parsley, hot pepper sauce, salt, and black pepper. Reduce the heat to low and simmer, uncovered, for 20 minutes.

3 Add the okra and shrimp and simmer for another 10 minutes.

4 Discard the bay leaf, ladle the gumbo into 4 bowls, and serve.

**HEALTH NOTE** | *This version of a New Orleans staple is just as authentic, but contains far less fat. If you prefer, you may omit the meat altogether.*

---

**SERVES: 4**

4 oz. turkey sausage

1 tbsp. canola oil

2 tbsp. unbleached all-purpose flour

1 can (28 oz.) plum tomatoes, with their liquid

1 medium onion, coarsely chopped

1 small green bell pepper, coarsely chopped

1 stalk celery, chopped

1/2 tsp. dried thyme

1 bay leaf

2 tbsp. chopped fresh parsley

1/4 tsp. hot pepper sauce, or to taste

1/4 tsp. salt

1/4 tsp. black pepper

10 oz. fresh or frozen whole okra, trimmed

8 oz. small, raw shrimp, peeled and deveined

---

DIABETIC EXCHANGE: 1/4 STARCH  3 1/2 VEGETABLE  1 1/2 FAT  1 1/2 VERY LEAN MEAT

CALORIES: 230  FAT: 8 G  SAT. FAT: 1 G  CARBOHYDRATES: 23 G  PROTEIN: 18 G  CHOLESTEROL: 85 MG  SODIUM: 733 MG  FIBER: 5 G

PEARS

BLUE CHEESE

BELGIAN ENDIVE

1 For the dressing, peel and core ½ of a pear. Puree the pear in a blender with 2 tablespoons of the lemon juice, apple juice, chives, and yogurt.

2 Halve, stem, and core but do not peel the remaining pears. Cut the pears lengthwise into ¼-inch-thick slices, and toss them with the remaining lemon juice in a medium bowl.

3 Line a serving platter with the endive leaves and arrange the pear slices on top. Crumble the cheese over the pears and drizzle with the dressing.

TIP | *When choosing Belgian endive, look for light-colored leaves that are tight and firm, then use it as soon as possible, within a few days of purchase.*

**SERVES: 4**

5 medium pears

3 tbsp. lemon juice

3 tbsp. apple juice

1 tbsp. chopped fresh chives

1 tbsp. plain nonfat yogurt

6 oz. Belgian endive, separated into leaves

1 oz. Gorgonzola cheese or other blue cheese

DIABETIC EXCHANGE: 2¼ FRUIT ¼ VEGETABLE ¼ HIGH-FAT MEAT

CALORIES: 164 FAT: 3 G SAT. FAT: 2 G CARBOHYDRATES: 35 G PROTEIN: 3 G CHOLESTEROL: 6 MG SODIUM: 106 MG FIBER: 6 G

1 Toss together the jicama, lime juice, and salt in a medium bowl. Let it sit at room temperature for 1 hour, tossing occasionally. Add the oranges, cayenne, and cilantro and toss. Let the mixture sit at least 15 minutes, preferably 2 hours.

2 Line a large bowl or platter with the lettuce, top with the salad, and serve.

**TIP** | *When choosing jicama, look for smooth, firm skin that is free of spots. Crunchy and sweet, this large, round, brown-skinned vegetable—also known as the Mexican potato—can now be found in many grocery stores. It is best eaten uncooked in salads like this one.*

**SERVES: 6**

1 medium jicama, peeled and diced

¼ cup fresh lime juice

Salt to taste

2 navel oranges, sectioned and diced

Cayenne or crushed red pepper to taste

2 tbsp. chopped fresh cilantro

1 head leaf lettuce, or 2 cups baby salad greens

DIABETIC EXCHANGE: ⅓ FRUIT  2 VEGETABLE

CALORIES: **69**   FAT: **.2 G**   SAT. FAT: **0 G**   CARBOHYDRATES: **17 G**   PROTEIN: **2 G**   CHOLESTEROL: **0 MG**   SODIUM: **7 MG**   FIBER: **7 G**

**SERVES: 2**

2 large cucumbers

½ cup plain nonfat yogurt

¼ cup chopped fresh mint,
  or 1 tbsp. dried mint

3 tbsp. lemon juice

4 plum tomatoes

4 oz. romaine lettuce, torn
  into bite-size pieces

¼ cup chopped scallions

1 oz. feta cheese, crumbled

2 Kalamata olives

1  Peel the cucumbers and halve them lengthwise. Seed one cucumber half, cut it into large chunks, and puree in a food processor or blender until smooth. Add the yogurt, mint, and lemon juice and process until well combined.

2  Cut the remaining cucumber halves lengthwise into quarters, then cut crosswise into ¼-inch-thick slices. Cut the tomatoes into large dice. Toss the romaine, cucumber, tomatoes, scallions, feta, and dressing together in a large bowl. Garnish each serving with an olive.

**HEALTH NOTE** | *Romaine lettuce contains roughly six times the amount of vitamin C found in iceberg lettuce. To keep it fresh, wrap the leaves in damp paper towels and store loosely in a plastic bag in the refrigerator. It's best used within 2 or 3 days of purchase.*

DIABETIC EXCHANGE: 4 VEGETABLE   ¼ FAT   ½ HIGH-FAT MEAT

CALORIES: 163   FAT: 5 G   SAT. FAT: 2 G   CARBOHYDRATES: 23 G   PROTEIN: 9 G   CHOLESTEROL: 14 MG   SODIUM: 330 MG   FIBER: 4 G

KALAMATA OLIVES

FETA CHEESE

MINT

**SERVES: 6**

½ cup fat-free, reduced-sodium chicken broth

1 tbsp. sesame seeds

1 tbsp. tahini (sesame paste)

1 tsp. toasted sesame oil

1½ tbsp. reduced-sodium soy sauce

1 tbsp. fresh lemon juice

1 tsp. minced, peeled fresh ginger

1 lb. spinach, washed, stemmed, and dried

¼ lb. mushrooms, wiped clean and thinly sliced (about 1 cup)

1 large ripe tomato, cut into thin wedges

⅛ tsp. salt

Freshly ground black pepper

1 Boil the broth in a small saucepan until only 2 tablespoons remain, about 7 minutes.

2 While the broth is reducing, toast the sesame seeds in a small, heavy-bottomed skillet over medium-low heat until they are golden, about 3 minutes. Set the skillet aside.

3 Whisk together the tahini and sesame oil in a small bowl. Whisk in the reduced broth, the soy sauce, lemon juice, and ginger.

4 Combine the spinach, mushrooms, and tomato in a large bowl. Add the dressing, salt, and black pepper to taste and toss well. Scatter the sesame seeds over the salad and serve.

**HEALTH NOTE** | *The sesame seeds, paste, and oil in this salad combine to provide respectable doses of calcium, protein, vitamin E, and iron. Look for dark sesame oil, which is made with roasted seeds, providing an intense sesame flavor. Tahini, a creamy spread made from ground sesame seeds, can be found in most grocery stores with other nut butters.*

DIABETIC EXCHANGE: 1¼ VEGETABLE ½ FAT

CALORIES: 59    FAT: 3 G    SAT. FAT: .4 G    CARBOHYDRATES: 6 G    PROTEIN: 3 G    CHOLESTEROL: 0 MG    SODIUM: 301 MG    FIBER: 3 G

1 Cut one of the cucumbers into thin slices and set the slices aside. Peel and seed the remaining cucumbers and chop finely. Place on a large square of doubled cheesecloth, gather the ends, and twist to wring out as much moisture as possible from the cucumbers. Discard the juice.

2 Combine the chopped cucumbers, tomato, dill, yogurt, sour cream, salt, and some pepper with the chickpeas, and gently toss the mixture. Serve the salad garnished with the reserved cucumber slices.

**HEALTH NOTE** | *Because of their high fiber content, chickpeas, like other beans, are digested slowly, making you feel full longer and easing the urge to snack. Beans also raise blood sugar levels less than any other carbohydrate-rich food.*

**SERVES: 6**

4 cucumbers (about 1½ lb.)

1 large tomato, peeled, seeded, and coarsely chopped

¼ cup fresh dill

½ cup plain low-fat yogurt

2 tbsp. sour cream

¼ tsp. salt

Freshly ground black pepper

2 cups canned chickpeas, drained and rinsed

DIABETIC EXCHANGE: ¾ STARCH   1 VEGETABLE   ½ FAT   ¼ VERY LEAN MEAT

CALORIES: **110**   FAT: **3 G**   SAT. FAT: **.9 G**   CARBOHYDRATES: **16 G**   PROTEIN: **5 G**   CHOLESTEROL: **3 MG**   SODIUM: **227 MG**   FIBER: **4 G**

# Sweet and Spicy Corn Salad

**SERVES: 12**

5 cups fresh corn kernels (cut from about 5 large ears), or 5 cups frozen corn kernels, thawed

¼ cup red wine vinegar

1 tbsp. brown sugar

2 tbsp. canola oil

2 tsp. chopped fresh oregano, or ½ tsp. dried oregano

¼ tsp. salt

Freshly ground black pepper

1 red bell pepper, seeded, deribbed, and cut into thin strips

1 green bell pepper, seeded, deribbed, and cut into thin strips

2 small jalapeño peppers, seeded and finely chopped

4 scallions, chopped

1 Combine the corn and just enough water to cover in a saucepan and simmer, covered, for 3 minutes; drain well.

2 Whisk together the vinegar, sugar, oil, oregano, salt, and black pepper.

3 Add the corn, red, green, and jalapeño peppers, and scallions, and toss the salad well.

4 Serve at room temperature or chilled.

**TIP** *Use care with jalapeños and other hot peppers. Avoid touching your face, lips, or eyes after you've cut them. The bell and hot peppers provide ample amounts of vitamin C and, at the same time, add a burst of sweet and spicy flavor.*

DIABETIC EXCHANGE: ⅔ STARCH   1 VEGETABLE   ½ FAT

CALORIES: 88   FAT: 3 G   SAT. FAT: .3 G   CARBOHYDRATES: 15 G   PROTEIN: 2 G   CHOLESTEROL: 0 MG   SODIUM: 59 MG   FIBER: 2 G

ROASTED PEPPERS

OLIVES

FRESH PARSLEY

1 Cook the onion, garlic, and oil in a skillet over moderate heat, stirring, until soft, about 5 minutes. Add the wine and boil until almost all of the liquid has evaporated. Add the broth, vinegar, salt, cumin, paprika, cloves, and crushed red pepper and simmer for 2 minutes. Remove the skillet from the heat.

2 Add the chickpeas and potatoes and toss gently. Add the pepper strips, olives, scallions, and parsley and toss again. Serve the salad at room temperature.

**HEALTH NOTE** | *This satisfying salad has loads of fiber, vitamin C, and vitamin $B_6$, yet is low in calories. Remember to store potatoes in a cool, dry place—but not the refrigerator. Refrigeration converts the starch in potatoes to sugar, making them undesirably sweet and causing them to darken when cooked.*

**SERVES: 4**

½ cup chopped onion

2 cloves garlic, chopped

1 tbsp. olive oil

2 tbsp. white wine

3 tbsp. fat-free, reduced-sodium chicken broth

2 tbsp. red wine vinegar

¼ tsp. salt

1 tsp. ground cumin

¼ tsp. paprika

⅛ tsp. ground cloves

Pinch of crushed red pepper

⅔ cup canned chickpeas, rinsed and drained

4 medium-size potatoes (2 lb.), boiled and cut into 1-inch pieces

½ cup bottled, sliced, roasted red bell peppers or pimentos, drained

4 black olives, pitted and halved

¼ cup chopped scallions

1½ tbsp. chopped fresh parsley

DIABETIC EXCHANGE: 2¾ STARCH   1 VEGETABLE   ¾ FAT

CALORIES: 269   FAT: 5 G   SAT. FAT: .6 G   CARBOHYDRATES: 52 G   PROTEIN: 6 G   CHOLESTEROL: 0 MG   SODIUM: 304 MG   FIBER: 5 G

**SERVES: 5**

3 oz. dried linguine or fettuccine, broken into 3-inch lengths

2 large carrots, cut into julienne strips

2 tbsp. rice vinegar or wine vinegar

1 tbsp. reduced-sodium soy sauce

1 tbsp. honey

1 tbsp. canola oil

¼ tsp. dry mustard

¼ tsp. toasted sesame oil

Dash of hot pepper sauce

3 cups shredded Chinese cabbage or spinach

2 tsp. toasted sesame seeds

1 Cook the pasta in a pot of boiling salted water for 5 minutes. Add the carrots and boil until the pasta is al dente. Drain in a colander and rinse under cold running water.

2 Combine the vinegar, soy sauce, honey, canola oil, mustard, sesame oil, and hot pepper sauce in a medium bowl. Add the pasta mixture; toss gently. Cover and chill in the refrigerator at least 2 hours, or up to 24 hours.

3 Add the cabbage before serving; toss gently. Sprinkle with the sesame seeds.

**HEALTH NOTE** | *Dairy products are not the only source of calcium. The Chinese cabbage or spinach in this salad both provide lots of this bone-building mineral as well as being packed with fiber.*

DIABETIC EXCHANGE: ¾ STARCH    ¼ CARBOHYDRATE    1¼ VEGETABLE    ¾ FAT

CALORIES: 136    FAT: 4 G    SAT. FAT: .4 G    CARBOHYDRATES: 22 G    PROTEIN: 4 G    CHOLESTEROL: 0 MG    SODIUM: 199 MG    FIBER: 3 G

# Tabbouleh Salad with Orange and Mint Dressing

**SERVES: 4**

½ cup frozen peas

1 cup bulgur

2 tsp. freshly grated orange zest

⅓ cup freshly squeezed orange juice

2 tbsp. olive oil

¼ tsp. freshly ground black pepper

Pinch of salt

1 cup thinly sliced red bell pepper

2 tbsp. chopped fresh mint,
  or 2 tsp. dried mint

1 Combine 1 cup of water and the peas in a saucepan and bring to a boil. Remove from the heat and stir in the bulgur. Cover and refrigerate for 30 minutes.

2 Transfer the bulgur to a large serving bowl. Add the orange zest and juice, oil, black pepper, salt, red pepper, and mint, and toss well.

DIABETIC EXCHANGE: **2** STARCH   ¼ VEGETABLE   **1¼** FAT

CALORIES: **212**   FAT: **7 G**   SAT. FAT: **1 G**   CARBOHYDRATES: **33 G**   PROTEIN: **6 G**   CHOLESTEROL: **0 MG**   SODIUM: **63 MG**   FIBER: **8 G**

ORANGE ZEST

MINT

OLIVE OIL

**SERVES: 6**

1½ cups fat-free, reduced-sodium chicken broth

¼ cup chopped shallot

2½ tbsp. fresh lemon juice

Freshly ground black pepper

1 cup couscous

⅓ cup coarsely chopped cilantro

1½ tbsp. olive oil

¼ lb. shiitake, oyster, or other wild mushrooms, wiped clean and sliced

1 tsp. fresh thyme, or ¼ tsp. dried thyme leaves

¼ lb. snow peas, stems and strings removed, each cut diagonally into 3 pieces

¼ tsp. salt

1 tsp. red wine vinegar

1 head red leaf lettuce, washed and dried

1 Bring the broth to a boil in a large saucepan with 2 tablespoons of shallots, 2 tablespoons of lemon juice, and some pepper. Stir in the couscous and half the cilantro. Cover the pan and remove it from the heat; let it stand while you complete the salad.

2 Heat 1 tablespoon of oil in a large skillet over medium-high heat. Add the mushrooms, thyme, and the remaining shallots. Sauté the mushrooms until they begin to brown, about 4 minutes. Stir in the snow peas, salt, and some pepper. Cook the mixture, stirring frequently, for 2 minutes.

3 Combine the vinegar and the remaining oil, lemon juice, and cilantro in a large bowl. Add the couscous, fluffing and stirring it with a fork until coated with the dressing. Add the vegetables and any juices in the skillet and toss. Cover and refrigerate the salad; serve on lettuce leaves.

**EDITOR'S NOTE** | *Couscous is finely cracked wheat that has been steamed, dried, and partly refined, although it still retains some fiber and vitamins. Mild-tasting, it picks up the flavors of whatever you pair it with; here, wild mushrooms give it a hearty, earthy taste.*

DIABETIC EXCHANGE: 1½ STARCH    1½ VEGETABLE    ½ FAT

CALORIES: 175    FAT: 4 G    SAT. FAT: .5 G    CARBOHYDRATES: 29 G    PROTEIN: 6 G    CHOLESTEROL: 0 MG    SODIUM: 259 MG    FIBER: 2 G

1  Cook the potatoes in a pot of boiling water until firm-tender, about 10 minutes. Drain and cool.

2  Bring the broth and rosemary to a boil in a large skillet over medium heat. Add the chicken and simmer, covered, until the chicken is cooked through, about 10 minutes. Transfer the chicken to a cutting board. (Reserve the broth for another use.) When cool enough to handle, cut the chicken on the diagonal into $\frac{1}{2}$-inch slices.

3  Cut 2 of the tomatoes into 6 wedges each and add to a large bowl with the potatoes, watercress, and chicken. Combine the lime juice, oil, and salt in a small bowl. Finely chop the 2 remaining tomatoes and add to the lime mixture. Pour all but $\frac{1}{4}$ cup of the tomato dressing over the salad and toss to combine.

4  Place the salad on a large platter, top with the reserved tomato dressing and the avocado; serve warm, at room temperature, or chilled.

**SERVES: 4**

$\frac{1}{4}$ lb. small red potatoes, quartered

1 cup fat-free, reduced-sodium chicken broth

$\frac{1}{4}$ tsp. dried rosemary, crumbled

10 oz. skinless, boneless chicken breasts

4 tomatoes

2 bunches (6 oz. each) of watercress, tough stems removed

$\frac{1}{4}$ cup fresh lime juice

1 tbsp. olive oil, preferably extra virgin

$\frac{1}{2}$ tsp. salt

$\frac{1}{3}$ cup diced avocado

**HEALTH NOTE** | *Avocados, once thought to be a "no-no" because of their fat content, taste deliciously sinful but are actually good for you. They are high in fiber, a good source of monounsaturated fat, and contain a substance called beta itosterol, which seems to improve cholesterol levels and fight cancer.*

DIABETIC EXCHANGE: $\frac{1}{4}$ STARCH   2 VEGETABLE   1 FAT   2$\frac{1}{4}$ VERY LEAN MEAT

CALORIES: **194**   FAT: **7 G**   SAT. FAT: **1 G**   CARBOHYDRATES: **14 G**   PROTEIN: **21 G**   CHOLESTEROL: **41 MG**   SODIUM: **540 MG**   FIBER: **4 G**

PEANUTS

GINGER

WATER CHESTNUTS

1 Preheat the broiler.

2 Combine the hoisin sauce, apple juice, oil, and salt in a large bowl. Place the chicken on a broiler rack and brush with 2 tablespoons of the hoisin mixture. Broil the chicken 4 inches from the heat for 4 minutes per side, or until just cooked through. Transfer the chicken to a cutting board and cut it into thin slices.

3 Add the chicken, bell peppers, carrots, sprouts, water chestnuts, scallion, and ginger to the remaining hoisin mixture and toss to coat.

4 Serve the salad on a bed of romaine, sprinkled with peanuts.

**HEALTH NOTE** *This warm chicken salad is a change from everyday mayonnaise-based chicken salads and can be served as an entrée. The peppers, bean sprouts, and romaine help supply your vegetable requirement for the day and are high in fiber and antioxidants.*

**SERVES: 4**

⅓ cup hoisin sauce

¼ cup apple juice

1 tsp. canola oil

¼ tsp. salt

1 lb. skinless, boneless chicken breasts

2 red bell peppers, cut into thin strips

2 carrots, shredded

2 cups mung bean sprouts

1 can (5 oz.) sliced water chestnuts, rinsed and drained

2 tbsp. finely chopped scallion

½ tsp. dried ground ginger

3 cups shredded romaine lettuce

1 tbsp. chopped, unsalted, dry-roasted peanuts

DIABETIC EXCHANGE: **1** CARBOHYDRATE **2¾** VEGETABLE **½** FAT **3½** VERY LEAN MEAT

CALORIES: **282** FAT: **4 G** SAT. FAT: **.6 G** CARBOHYDRATES: **29 G** PROTEIN: **30 G** CHOLESTEROL: **66 MG** SODIUM: **657 MG** FIBER: **4 G**

# Caesar Salad with Grilled Chicken Breasts

**SERVES: 4**

4 oz. Italian or French bread, cut into ½-inch slices

2 cloves garlic, peeled and halved

¼ tsp. salt

½ tsp. dried oregano

¼ tsp. freshly ground black pepper

3 tbsp. fresh lemon juice

1 lb. skinless, boneless chicken breasts

½ cup fat-free, reduced-sodium chicken broth

3 tbsp. reduced-fat mayonnaise

1 tbsp. reduced-fat sour cream

1 tbsp. anchovy paste

5 cups torn romaine lettuce

8 cherry tomatoes, halved

1 tbsp. capers, drained

1 Preheat the oven to 400°.

2 Place the bread on a baking sheet and bake for 5 minutes, or until crisp and golden. Immediately rub the toast with the cut sides of the garlic. Cut the bread into cubes for croutons and set aside.

3 Preheat the broiler or prepare the grill.

4 Combine the salt, oregano, pepper, and 1 tablespoon of lemon juice in a small bowl. Rub the mixture onto the chicken and broil or grill 6 inches from the heat for about 5 minutes per side, or until cooked through. When cool enough to handle, cut the chicken into strips.

5 Whisk together the broth, mayonnaise, sour cream, anchovy paste, and the remaining lemon juice in a large bowl. Add the lettuce, cherry tomatoes, capers, and croutons and toss well. Serve the salad, topped with the sliced chicken, warm or at room temperature.

**HEALTH NOTE** *The garlic toast in this salad contains none of the butter or oil of traditional croutons but tastes just as good.*

**TIP** *You can rub the spice mixture onto the chicken up to 2 hours in advance, then keep the chicken refrigerated until ready to cook.*

DIABETIC EXCHANGE: 1 STARCH  1¼ VEGETABLE  1 FAT  3¼ VERY LEAN MEAT

CALORIES: 271  FAT: 6 G  SAT. FAT: 1 G  CARBOHYDRATES: 21 G  PROTEIN: 31 G  CHOLESTEROL: 68 MG  SODIUM: 865 MG  FIBER: 4 G

# Thai Lemon-Lime Shrimp Salad

1  Put the apple slivers in a large bowl and toss with the lemon and lime juices, shallots, cilantro, mint, fish or soy sauce, garlic, pepper flakes, and scallions.

2  Cook the shrimp in a pot of boiling salted water until they are just cooked through, about 1 minute; drain and add to the bowl. Toss the salad gently, cover the bowl, and chill in the refrigerator for at least 30 minutes.

3  Serve the salad on lettuce leaves, garnished with a sprig of mint.

**HEALTH NOTE** | *Fish sauce, a pungent, salty, condiment found in many Asian grocery shops, is actually a good source of B vitamins. Asian cooks consider it an indispensable ingredient and use it much as soy sauce is used.*

---

**SERVES: 4**
**(as a main course)**

1 Granny Smith apple, peeled, cored, and cut into slivers

3 tbsp. fresh lemon juice

3 tbsp. fresh lime juice

2 shallots, thinly sliced

1½ tbsp. chopped cilantro

1 tbsp. chopped fresh mint, or 1 tsp. dried mint

2 tsp. fish sauce or reduced-sodium soy sauce

2 cloves garlic, finely chopped

¼ tsp. red pepper flakes, or to taste

2 scallions, thinly sliced

1 lb. medium shrimp, peeled, halved lengthwise, and deveined

2 heads of Boston lettuce, or 4 heads of Bibb lettuce, washed and dried

4 mint sprigs

---

DIABETIC EXCHANGE: ⅓ FRUIT   1¼ VEGETABLE   ¼ FAT   2½ VERY LEAN MEAT

CALORIES: **148**   FAT: **2 G**   SAT. FAT: **.4 G**   CARBOHYDRATES: **12 G**   PROTEIN: **21 G**   CHOLESTEROL: **140 MG**   SODIUM: **242 MG**   FIBER: **2 G**

# White Bean, Tuna, and Tomato Salad

**SERVES: 4**

⅓ cup chopped scallions

1 tsp. grated lemon zest

2 tbsp. fresh lemon juice

1 tbsp. white wine vinegar

1 tbsp. olive oil

2 cups halved cherry tomatoes

1 can (16 oz.) cannellini beans
or other white beans, rinsed
and drained

1 can (6 oz.) water-packed, albacore
tuna, drained and flaked

3 tbsp. minced fresh basil

4 large leaves red leaf lettuce

1  Whisk together the scallions, zest, lemon juice, vinegar, and oil in a
large bowl.

2  Add the tomatoes, beans, tuna, and basil. Toss gently and refrigerate the
salad, covered, for at least 30 minutes. Serve on lettuce-lined plates.

**HEALTH NOTE** | *Tuna is especially high in omega-3 fatty acids, which seem to play a
role in lowering heart attack risk. Keep the basic ingredients for this nutritious and
flavorful salad on hand for a quick, last-minute meal.*

DIABETIC EXCHANGE: ¾ STARCH   ¾ VEGETABLE   ¾ FAT   1½ VERY LEAN MEAT

CALORIES: **166**   FAT: **5 G**   SAT. FAT: **.8 G**   CARBOHYDRATES: **15 G**   PROTEIN: **16 G**   CHOLESTEROL: **17 MG**   SODIUM: **346 MG**   FIBER: **4 G**

CANNELLINI

BASIL

TUNA

# Penne Rigati with Mushrooms and Tarragon

**SERVES: 4**

2 tbsp. (½ oz.) dried
    porcini mushrooms

2 tbsp. olive oil

1 small onion, finely chopped

½ lb. button mushrooms,
    cut into ¼-inch dice

½ tsp. salt

Freshly ground black pepper

3 cloves garlic, finely chopped

1 cup dry white wine

8 oz. penne rigati (or other short,
    tubular pasta)

1½ lb. tomatoes, peeled, seeded,
    and chopped (about 2 cups)

½ cup chopped fresh parsley

2 tbsp. chopped fresh tarragon

1 Pour 1 cup of hot water over the dried mushrooms and soak them until they are soft—about 20 minutes. Drain them and reserve their soaking liquid. Cut the drained porcini into ¼-inch pieces.

2 Heat the oil in a large skillet over medium heat. Add the onion and sauté it until it turns translucent, about 4 minutes. Add the porcini and button mushrooms, salt, and pepper and cook until the mushrooms begin to brown, about 5 minutes. Add the garlic and the wine, and boil the mixture until the liquid is reduced to about 2 tablespoons, about 5 minutes more.

3 Cook the penne rigati in a pot of boiling, salted water until it is al dente—8 to 10 minutes.

4 While the penne rigati is cooking, pour the reserved porcini-soaking liquid into the skillet containing the mushrooms and boil until the liquid is reduced to about ¼ cup, about 5 minutes. Stir in the tomatoes and cook the mixture until it is heated through.

5 Drain the pasta and add it to the skillet with the chopped parsley and tarragon. Toss well and serve.

TIP | *Dried porcini mushrooms are available in most gourmet grocery stores, and their rich flavor makes them worth looking for. Choose mushrooms that are a tan to a pale brown in color. Avoid those that appear crumbly. Dried mushrooms will last for many months in your pantry. Olives make a great garnish for this dish.*

DIABETIC EXCHANGE: 2¾ STARCH    2½ VEGETABLE    1½ FAT

CALORIES: 351    FAT: 8 G    SAT. FAT: 1 G    CARBOHYDRATES: 58 G    PROTEIN: 11 G    CHOLESTEROL: 0 MG    SODIUM: 511 MG    FIBER: 6 G

**SERVES: 4**

1½ lb. ripe tomatoes, peeled
and chopped, seeds and juice
reserved, or 1 can (28 oz.)
no-salt-added whole tomatoes,
drained and chopped

1 onion, chopped

1 carrot, chopped

1 tsp. fresh thyme, or ¼ tsp.
dried thyme leaves

1 tsp. chopped fresh rosemary,
or ¼ tsp. dried rosemary

¼ tsp. salt

Freshly ground black pepper

1 cup canned artichoke hearts
packed in water, drained
and quartered

1 tbsp. red wine vinegar or
cider vinegar

8 oz. fettuccine

¼ cup freshly grated Romano
or Parmesan cheese

1 Combine the chopped tomatoes with their juice, onion, carrot, thyme, rosemary, salt, and pepper in a saucepan and simmer the mixture for 5 minutes. Add the artichokes and vinegar and simmer until most of the liquid has evaporated, about 15 minutes.

2 Approximately 15 minutes before the vegetables are done, cook the fettuccine in a pot of boiling, salted water until it is al dente, about 8 to 10 minutes. Drain the fettuccine and add it immediately to the sauce. Sprinkle with the cheese, toss lightly, and serve.

**HEALTH NOTE** | *Artichokes are low in calories and contain ample amounts of potassium, calcium, phosphorus, and fiber. The artichoke hearts used here are the best part; they are rich in flavor and add body to the sauce.*

DIABETIC EXCHANGE: 2¾ STARCH    3½ VEGETABLE    ¼ FAT

CALORIES: 311    FAT: 3 G    SAT. FAT: 1 G    CARBOHYDRATES: 60 G    PROTEIN: 12 G    CHOLESTEROL: 5 MG    SODIUM: 422 MG    FIBER: 5 G

THYME

ROSEMARY

ROMANO CHEESE

# Spaghetti with Fresh Basil, Pine Nuts, and Cheese

1 Cook the garlic in the oil over medium heat in a large skillet, stirring constantly, for about 1 minute. Stir in the shredded basil leaves and the broth and simmer the liquid gently while you cook the pasta.

2 Cook the spaghetti in a pot of boiling, salted water until it is al dente, about 8 to 10 minutes. Drain the pasta and add it to the skillet.

3 Toss well to coat the pasta. Add the pine nuts, Romano, salt, and some pepper, and toss again. Serve immediately, garnished with the whole basil leaves.

---

**EDITOR'S NOTE** | *Pine nuts, also known as pignoli, actually grow inside the pine cone; they can be found in most grocery stores. For best flavor, toast them until they turn golden brown.*

**SERVES: 4**

1 clove garlic, crushed

1 tbsp. olive oil

1 cup shredded basil leaves plus several whole leaves reserved for garnish

½ cup fat-free, reduced-sodium chicken broth

8 oz. spaghetti

2 tbsp. toasted pine nuts

¼ cup freshly grated Romano cheese

¼ tsp. salt

Freshly ground black pepper

DIABETIC EXCHANGE: 2 ¾ STARCH    ¼ VEGETABLE    ½ FAT    ½ HIGH-FAT MEAT

CALORIES: 291    FAT: 8 G    SAT. FAT: 2 G    CARBOHYDRATES: 44 G    PROTEIN: 11 G    CHOLESTEROL: 5 MG    SODIUM: 479 MG    FIBER: 3 G

**SERVES: 8**

Red onions (about ¼ lb.),
  sliced into ½-inch-thick rounds

8 oz. lasagne

1¼ cups bottled, roasted,
  sliced red peppers

3 tsp. fresh thyme, or 1 tsp.
  dried thyme leaves

2 tbsp. olive oil

1 small head escarole (about 1 lb.),
  washed, trimmed, and sliced
  crosswise into 1-inch-wide strips

¼ tsp. salt

Freshly ground black pepper

¼ cup freshly grated
  Parmesan cheese

4 oz. Gorgonzola cheese, broken
  into small pieces

**TIP** | *Escarole, a variety of endive, has a milder flavor than either Belgian or curly endive and is high in calcium. You may substitute spinach if you like.*

1 Preheat the broiler. Broil the onions on a baking sheet, turning occasionally, until they are lightly browned—10 to 15 minutes. Separate the onion slices into rings and reserve.

2 Cook the lasagne in a large pot of boiling water for 7 minutes; the pasta will be slightly underdone. Drain the pasta and rinse in cold running water.

3 Puree ¼ cup of the red peppers in a food processor or blender with the pepper juices and 2 teaspoons of fresh thyme or ½ teaspoon of dried thyme.

4 Preheat the oven to 350°. Heat the oil in a large skillet over medium-high heat and sauté the escarole, ¼ teaspoon salt, the remaining thyme, and some black pepper until the escarole is wilted and almost all the liquid has evaporated, about 5 minutes. Remove the pan from the heat.

5 Line the bottom of a 9-by-11-inch baking dish with a layer of the lasagne. Top with half of the escarole and 1 tablespoon of the Parmesan, half of the remaining pepper strips, and half of the onion rings. Build a second layer the same way, this time topping the onion with half of the pepper puree. Cover with a final layer of lasagne, and spread the remaining puree on top. Scatter the Gorgonzola evenly over the pepper puree and sprinkle with the remaining Parmesan.

6 Bake the lasagne for 30 minutes. Let the dish stand for 10 minutes to allow the flavors to meld.

DIABETIC EXCHANGE: 1¼ STARCH    1 VEGETABLE    1 FAT

CALORIES: 221    FAT: 9 G    SAT. FAT: 4 G    CARBOHYDRATES: 27 G    PROTEIN: 9 G    CHOLESTEROL: 15 MG    SODIUM: 379 MG    FIBER: 2 G

GORGONZOLA

ESCAROLE

ROASTED PEPPERS

1 Cook the garlic in the oil in a large skillet over medium heat for 30 seconds. Add the tomatoes, capers, olives, crushed red pepper, and salt; simmer, partially covered, for 20 minutes. Add the oregano and simmer 10 minutes more.

2 Cook the linguine in a pot of boiling, salted water until it is al dente, about 8 to 10 minutes. Drain the pasta and add it to the skillet, tossing to coat it with the sauce. Top with the Romano and serve.

**EDITOR'S NOTE** | *Capers are the flower buds of a bush native to the Mediter-ranean and parts of Asia. They come pickled in a strong brine so make sure to rinse them prior to use to remove the salt. Although olives are very high in fat, it is monounsaturated, and the oil-cured ones have such intense flavor that this recipe requires only six.*

**SERVES: 4**

1 clove garlic, very finely chopped

1 tbsp. olive oil

2½ lb. ripe tomatoes, peeled, seeded, and chopped, or 1 can (28 oz.) no-salt-added whole tomatoes, drained and chopped

2 tsp. capers, drained, rinsed, and chopped

6 oil-cured olives, pitted and cut lengthwise into strips

⅛ tsp. crushed red pepper

¼ tsp. salt

1 tsp. chopped fresh oregano, or ½ tsp. dried oregano

8 oz. linguine

2 tbsp. freshly grated Romano cheese

DIABETIC EXCHANGE: 2¾ STARCH    2½ VEGETABLE    1¼ FAT

CALORIES: **319**   FAT: **7 G**   SAT. FAT: **1 G**   CARBOHYDRATES: **55 G**   PROTEIN: **10 G**   CHOLESTEROL: **3 MG**   SODIUM: **382 MG**   FIBER: **5 G**

WHITE WINE

TOMATOES

CHILI PEPPERS

1 Combine the tomatoes, chili peppers, and ¼ cup of water and cook over medium heat until the tomatoes have rendered their juice and most of the liquid has evaporated, about 20 minutes. Press the mixture through a sieve and set aside.

2 Cook the penne in a pot of boiling, salted water until it is al dente — 10 to 15 minutes.

3 While the pasta is cooking, heat the oil in a large skillet over medium-high heat and cook the onion, stirring constantly, until it turns translucent — 3 to 5 minutes. Add the mushrooms, bacon, and garlic; sauté for 5 minutes. Add the wine and boil until the liquid is reduced by half, about 3 minutes. Stir in the reserved tomato mixture and the parsley, and keep the sauce warm.

4 Drain the pasta, transfer it to a platter or bowl, and toss with the butter and the sauce; serve immediately.

**HEALTH NOTE** | *Canadian bacon has about 10 percent of the fat in regular bacon. If you cannot find Canadian bacon, substitute lean cooked ham.*

**SERVES: 8**

2½ lb. fresh Italian plum tomatoes, quartered, or 1 can (28 oz.) no-salt-added whole tomatoes, drained

4 whole, dried red chili peppers

1 lb. penne (or other tubular pasta)

2 tbsp. olive oil

1 onion, finely chopped

1 lb. mushrooms, wiped clean and sliced

2 oz. Canadian bacon, cut into small strips

4 cloves garlic, finely chopped

½ cup dry white wine

2 tbsp. chopped fresh parsley, preferably Italian

1 tbsp. unsalted butter

DIABETIC EXCHANGE: 2¾ STARCH   2 VEGETABLE   1 FAT   ¼ LEAN MEAT

CALORIES: 322   FAT: 7 G   SAT. FAT: 2 G   CARBOHYDRATES: 55 G   PROTEIN: 12 G   CHOLESTEROL: 7 MG   SODIUM: 315 MG   FIBER: 5 G

Ziti with Italian Sausage and **Red Peppers**

**SERVES: 4**

2 Italian-style turkey sausage links (about 4 oz.)

2 cloves garlic, finely chopped

2 tsp. fresh thyme, or ½ tsp. dried thyme leaves

8 oz. ziti (or other tubular pasta)

3 bottled roasted red peppers

1 large tomato, peeled, seeded, and pureed

1 tbsp. red wine vinegar

⅛ tsp. salt

1 Squeeze the sausages out of their casings and brown the meat, breaking it up, in a skillet over medium-high heat for about 3 minutes. Remove the pan from the heat and stir in the garlic and thyme.

2 Cook the pasta in a pot of boiling, salted water until it is al dente— 10 to 15 minutes.

3 While the pasta is cooking, slice the peppers lengthwise into thin strips.

4 Set the skillet containing the sausage mixture over medium heat. Add the pepper strips and reserved juices, the pureed tomato, the vinegar, and salt. Simmer the sauce until it thickens and is reduced by about one-third— 5 to 7 minutes.

5 Drain the pasta, return it to the pot, and combine it with the sauce. Cover the pot and let the pasta stand for 5 minutes to allow the flavors to blend.

**HEALTH NOTE** | *Pasta is relatively low in calories (about 210 per cup), easy to pre-pare, inexpensive, and versatile. People with diabetes may eat all carbohydrates as long as they are carefully measured and counted as part of the overall daily plan. This simple recipe gets all its flavor from smoky, roasted red peppers, fresh tomato, and a small amount of spicy sausage that adds very little fat.*

DIABETIC EXCHANGE: **2 ½ STARCH**   **1 ½ VEGETABLE**   **¼ FAT**   **½ LEAN MEAT**

CALORIES: **286**   FAT: **4 G**   SAT. FAT: **1 G**   CARBOHYDRATES: **51 G**   PROTEIN: **12 G**   CHOLESTEROL: **15 MG**   SODIUM: **338 MG**   FIBER: **2 G**

**SERVES: 4**

⅓ cup sun-dried tomatoes
(not oil-packed)

1 medium eggplant (about 1 lb.),
cut lengthwise into ½-inch-
thick slices

2½ tbsp. olive oil

8 oz. fettuccine

1 large, ripe tomato, peeled
and seeded

1 shallot, finely chopped

1 clove garlic, finely chopped

1 tbsp. red wine vinegar

Freshly ground black pepper

¼ cup chopped fresh basil

1 Preheat the broiler. Combine the sun-dried tomatoes and enough boiling water to cover in a small bowl and let stand until the tomatoes have softened, about 15 minutes.

2 Brush both sides of the eggplant slices with 1½ tablespoons of the oil and cut each eggplant slice into cubes. Put the cubes on a baking sheet in a single layer and broil them until they are well browned, turning occasionally. Turn off the broiler, but leave the eggplant in the oven to keep it warm.

3 Cook the fettuccine in a pot of boiling, salted water until it is al dente, about 8 to 10 minutes.

4 While the pasta is cooking, puree the fresh tomato in a food processor or blender. Combine the tomato puree, drained sun-dried tomatoes, shallot, garlic, vinegar, the remaining tablespoon of oil, and a generous helping of pepper in a small saucepan, and simmer, stirring, for 2 minutes. Remove the pan from the heat and stir in the basil.

5 Drain the pasta and transfer it to a large serving bowl. Add the warm eggplant cubes and the sauce, toss well, and serve immediately.

**HEALTH NOTE** | *Eggplants are notorious oil sponges when fried or sautéed. When baked, as in this dish, they soften and brown beautifully with a modest amount of oil.*

DIABETIC EXCHANGE: 2¾ STARCH   3 VEGETABLE   1½ FAT

CALORIES: 347   FAT: 10 G   SAT. FAT: 1 G   CARBOHYDRATES: 56 G   PROTEIN: 10 G   CHOLESTEROL: 0 MG   SODIUM: 213 MG   FIBER: 5 G

# Indian-Spiced Monkfish

1   Puree the lemon juice, garlic, ginger, cilantro, coriander seeds, turmeric, brown sugar, cumin seeds, mustard seeds, and salt in a blender.

2   Cook the onion in 1 tablespoon of the oil in a heavy-bottomed skillet until it is translucent, about 4 minutes. Add the spice puree and cook for 3 minutes. Transfer the mixture to a bowl and stir in the yogurt.

3   Preheat the broiler.

4   Rinse the fish and pat it dry with paper towels. Slice the fillets crosswise into pieces about 2 inches wide. Coat the pieces with half of the yogurt mixture and dredge them in the breadcrumbs. Put the fish in a flame-proof baking dish and drizzle the remaining tablespoon of oil over it. Broil the fish 3 inches from the heat for about 3 minutes on each side.

5   Set the oven temperature to 450° and bake the fish until it feels firm to the touch, about 10 minutes. Serve the monkfish with the remaining yogurt sauce.

**EDITOR'S NOTE** | *Monkfish is low in fat and has been called "the poor man's lobster" because of its similarly mild, sweet flavor and firm texture.*

**SERVES: 4**

Juice of 2 lemons

4 cloves garlic, chopped

1 tbsp. chopped fresh ginger

2 tbsp. chopped cilantro

1 tsp. each: coriander seeds, ground turmeric, and dark brown sugar

½ tsp. cumin seeds

¼ tsp. mustard seeds

¼ tsp. salt

1 onion, finely chopped

2 tbsp. canola oil

¾ cup plain low-fat yogurt

1 lb. monkfish fillets

¾ cup dry breadcrumbs

DIABETIC EXCHANGE: **1** STARCH    **1½** VEGETABLE    **¼** LOW-FAT MILK    **1½** FAT    **2** VERY LEAN MEAT

CALORIES: **287**    FAT: **11 G**    SAT. FAT: **1 G**    CARBOHYDRATES: **26 G**    PROTEIN: **22 G**    CHOLESTEROL: **31 MG**    SODIUM: **371 MG**    FIBER: **2 G**

# Broiled Shrimp with Tomato-Ginger Sauce

**SERVES: 4**

24 medium shrimp (about 1 lb.), peeled and deveined

1 onion, chopped

½ cup dry white wine

2 tbsp. fresh lemon juice

2 tbsp. olive oil

3 scallions, trimmed and chopped

6 cloves garlic, chopped

1 tbsp. minced fresh ginger

2 jalapeño peppers, seeded and chopped

¼ tsp. each: ground coriander, cumin, and dry mustard

3 ripe tomatoes, peeled, seeded, and chopped

1 tsp. brown sugar

1 tbsp. red wine vinegar

1 Combine the shrimp, onion, wine, lemon juice, and 1 tablespoon of the oil in a bowl and marinate in the refrigerator for 1 hour.

2 Meanwhile, heat the rest of the oil in a large, heavy-bottomed skillet over medium-high heat. Add the scallions, garlic, ginger, and jalapeño peppers; cook for 2 minutes, stirring constantly. Stir in the coriander, cumin, and mustard; cook the mixture for 1 minute. Add the tomatoes and cook, stirring constantly, for 1 minute. Remove the skillet from the heat and stir in the brown sugar and vinegar. Transfer the sauce to a serving bowl and let it cool.

3 Preheat the broiler.

4 Thread the shrimp onto 4 skewers and broil until they are opaque, about 3 minutes. Serve the shrimp with the sauce.

**TIP** | *To mince ginger, peel the skin and then make several crosswise slices. Stack two slices and cut them into thin strips. Turn the strips and cut them into small pieces. Unpeeled and tightly wrapped, fresh ginger can stay fresh in the refrigerator for 3 weeks.*

DIABETIC EXCHANGE: **2¼ VEGETABLE**  **½ FAT**  **2¼ VERY LEAN MEAT**

CALORIES: **171**  FAT: **4 G**  SAT. FAT: **.6 G**  CARBOHYDRATES: **12 G**  PROTEIN: **20 G**  CHOLESTEROL: **140 MG**  SODIUM: **150 MG**  FIBER: **2 G**

SHRIMP

SCALLIONS

JALAPEÑO

1 Rinse the fish under cold running water and pat it dry with paper towels.

2 Heat the oil over medium heat in a heavy-bottomed skillet large enough to hold the fish in one layer. Add the red bell pepper and sauté it for 2 minutes. Add the garlic, jalapeño pepper, and chopped cilantro and cook, stirring, for 1 minute. Place the fish on the vegetables and sprinkle with salt, pepper, and paprika. Pour in the wine and bring the liquid to a simmer, basting the fish occasionally. Cover the skillet and cook the fish at a bare simmer until it is opaque, about 8 minutes.

3 With a slotted spatula, transfer the fish to a deep platter. Remove the skin from the fillets and keep the fish warm and covered. Boil the liquid in the skillet until it is reduced to about ½ cup. Pour the sauce over the fish and serve at room temperature or cold, garnished with the cilantro sprigs.

**SERVES: 4**

4 Pacific white sea bass or halibut fillets (4 oz. each)

2 tbsp. canola oil

2 red bell peppers, diced

20 cloves garlic, peeled and very thinly sliced

1 jalapeño pepper, seeded and finely chopped

6 tbsp. finely chopped cilantro plus several whole sprigs for garnish

¼ tsp. salt

Freshly ground black pepper

1 tsp. paprika, preferably Hungarian

2 cups dry white wine

**EDITOR'S NOTE** | *Those 20 cloves of garlic may sound like a lot, but rest assured that they'll mellow to a mild, earthy sweetness as they cook. Garlic contains sulfur compounds that may lower blood pressure and cholesterol levels.*

DIABETIC EXCHANGE: 1¾ VEGETABLE    1½ FAT    3 VERY LEAN MEAT

CALORIES: 222    FAT: 10 G    SAT. FAT: 1 G    CARBOHYDRATES: 9 G    PROTEIN: 25 G    CHOLESTEROL: 52 MG    SODIUM: 239 MG    FIBER: 1 G

# Grilled Halibut with Cucumber-Chive Sauce

**SERVES: 4**

1 tbsp. butter, melted

¼ cup snipped fresh chives
or scallions

½ tsp. salt

½ tsp. black pepper

2 halibut steaks (1 lb. total)

¼ cup low-fat sour cream

¾ cup plain low-fat yogurt

3 tbsp. lemon juice

2 tsp. grated lemon zest (optional)

½ tsp. dry mustard

¼ cup peeled, finely chopped
cucumber

¼ cup minced red bell pepper

1  Preheat a grill.

2  Combine the melted butter, 1 tablespoon of the chives, ¼ teaspoon of the salt, and ¼ teaspoon of the black pepper in a small bowl.

3  Grill the halibut for 5 minutes on each side, or until the fish is opaque and just flakes when tested with the tip of a knife.

4  Stir together the sour cream, yogurt, lemon juice, lemon zest (if using), mustard, the remaining 3 tablespoons of chives, ¼ teaspoon salt, ¼ teaspoon black pepper, the cucumber, and the bell pepper in a medium bowl.

5  Cut the halibut steaks in half, top with the butter mixture, and serve with the cucumber-chive sauce.

**TIP** | *You can substitute any firm white fish, like swordfish, for the halibut—or try salmon. The cucumber-chive sauce is also good as a dip for fresh vegetables or used to top a baked potato.*

DIABETIC EXCHANGE: 1¼ VEGETABLE  1 FAT  2¾ VERY LEAN MEAT

CALORIES: 179   FAT: 7 G   SAT. FAT: 3 G   CARBOHYDRATES: 7 G   PROTEIN: 22 G   CHOLESTEROL: 45 MG   SODIUM: 417 MG   FIBER: .3 G

MANGO

CILANTRO

FENNEL

1   Place the fennel seeds in a large, heavy-duty zip-top plastic bag. Seal the bag and finely crush the seeds using a meat mallet or a rolling pin.

2   Combine the crushed fennel seeds, cumin, coriander, paprika, and cayenne in a large nonstick skillet. Toast over medium heat, shaking the pan, until fragrant, about 2 minutes. Remove from heat; stir in the sugar and salt.

3   Combine 1 teaspoon of the spice mixture with the tomato, mango, papaya, cilantro, and lime juice in a bowl.

4   Place each chicken breast half between 2 sheets of heavy-duty plastic wrap and flatten to $\frac{1}{4}$-inch thickness using a meat mallet or rolling pin.

5   Sprinkle the chicken with the remaining spice mixture. Heat the oil in the nonstick skillet over medium-high heat. Sauté the chicken for 4 minutes on each side or until done. Top with the fruit salsa.

**HEALTH NOTE** | *The tomatoes, papaya, and mango used in the salsa provide ample beta carotene, and the tomato is also a source of lycopene, another powerful antioxidant. This brightly colored salsa can be served with grilled fish and seafood too.*

**SERVES: 4**

$1\frac{1}{2}$ tbsp. fennel seeds

1 tbsp. ground cumin

1 tsp. ground coriander

$\frac{1}{2}$ tsp. paprika

$\frac{1}{2}$ tsp. cayenne

1 tsp. sugar

$\frac{1}{4}$ tsp. salt

1 cup diced plum tomatoes

1 cup diced peeled mango

1 cup diced peeled papaya

1 tbsp. chopped fresh cilantro

1 tsp. lime juice

4 skinless, boneless chicken breast halves (4 oz. each)

1 tbsp. canola oil

DIABETIC EXCHANGE: $\frac{2}{3}$ FRUIT   **1** VEGETABLE   **1** FAT   $3\frac{1}{4}$ VERY LEAN MEAT

CALORIES: **224**   FAT: **6 G**   SAT. FAT: **.7 G**   CARBOHYDRATES: **16 G**   PROTEIN: **28 G**   CHOLESTEROL: **66 MG**   SODIUM: **228 MG**   FIBER: **2 G**

# Grilled Chicken Fajitas

**SERVES: 4**

2 tbsp. fresh lime juice

1 tbsp. chili powder

2 tsp. olive oil

¼ tsp. salt

¼ tsp. freshly ground
black pepper

1 lb. skinless, boneless
chicken breasts

1 lb. tomatoes, coarsely chopped

1 can (4½ oz.) chopped
mild green chilies, drained

½ cup chopped fresh cilantro

⅓ cup diced avocado

Eight 8-inch corn tortillas

4 cups shredded romaine lettuce

1 In a sturdy plastic bag, combine 1 tablespoon of the lime juice, the chili powder, oil, ¼ teaspoon of the salt, and the pepper. Add the chicken, squeeze the air out of the bag, seal, and marinate at room temperature for 30 minutes or up to 12 hours in the refrigerator.

2 In a medium bowl, combine the tomatoes, green chilies, cilantro, avocado, remaining 1 tablespoon lime juice, and remaining ¼ teaspoon salt.

3 Take the rack off the grill, spray it with cooking spray, then preheat the grill to a medium heat. Grill the chicken, covered, turning once, for 8 minutes, or until the chicken is cooked through. Place the tortillas on the grill for 30 seconds to warm through.

4 Thinly slice the chicken. Place 2 tortillas on each of the 4 plates, spoon the chicken slices onto the tortillas along with the tomato mixture and lettuce, and serve.

**HEALTH NOTE** | *Corn tortillas provide more fiber and nutrients than their flour counterparts, contain no fat, and are full of flavor.*

DIABETIC EXCHANGE: **2** STARCH  **2** VEGETABLE  **1** FAT  **3¼** VERY LEAN MEAT

CALORIES: **348**  FAT: **8 G**  SAT. FAT: **1 G**  CARBOHYDRATES: **39 G**  PROTEIN: **32 G**  CHOLESTEROL: **66 MG**  SODIUM: **544 MG**  FIBER: **7 G**

**SERVES: 4**

3 large grapefruit

1 tsp. fennel seeds

½ tsp. coarse ground
  black pepper

¼ tsp. salt

1 clove garlic, minced

4 skinless, boneless chicken
  breast halves (about 4 oz. each)

2 tbsp. all-purpose flour

1 tsp. olive oil

1 tbsp. brown sugar

¼ tsp. red pepper flakes

12 black olives, pitted
  and halved

1  Cut the rind off the grapefruit with a sharp knife. Working over a bowl
   to catch the juice, cut the grapefruit into sections. Squeeze the membranes
   to extract ½ cup juice and reserve.

2  Combine the fennel, black pepper, salt, and garlic in a small bowl. Rub
   the mixture evenly over the chicken and sprinkle with flour.

3  Heat the oil in a large nonstick skillet over medium-high heat. Sauté
   the chicken breast halves for 4 minutes on each side or until browned.

4  Transfer the chicken to a platter. Add the reserved grapefruit juice,
   sugar, and red pepper flakes to the skillet, scraping up the browned bits;
   cook for 1 minute. Return the chicken to the pan and simmer it, covered,
   for 12 minutes, or until the chicken is done. Stir in the grapefruit sections
   and olives and simmer for 1 minute.

**TIP** | *Select grapefruit with thin, fine-textured, brightly colored skin. The
fruit should be firm, yet springy when pressed. The heavier the fruit, the more
juice it yields.*

DIABETIC EXCHANGE: ¼ STARCH  1 FRUIT  2 VEGETABLE  ½ FAT  3¼ VERY LEAN MEAT

CALORIES: 263  FAT: 4 G  SAT. FAT: .7 G  CARBOHYDRATES: 29 G  PROTEIN: 28 G  CHOLESTEROL: 66 MG  SODIUM: 319 MG  FIBER: 2 G

1  Combine the chicken, chili powder, and cumin in a bowl and toss to coat.

2  Heat the oil in a large nonstick skillet over medium-high heat, add the onion, and sauté for 5 minutes. Add the chicken, bell pepper, and garlic and sauté for 3 minutes. Add the salsa, beer, tomatoes, and beans and cook for 10 minutes, or until the chicken is done.

3  Ladle the chili into 4 soup bowls and sprinkle it with the cheese. Garnish with fresh cilantro, if desired.

---

**HEALTH NOTE** | *This hearty chili provides plenty of fiber and antioxidants.*

**SERVES: 4**

¾ lb. skinless, boneless chicken breasts, cut into 1-inch pieces

1 tbsp. chili powder

1 tsp. ground cumin

1 tbsp. canola oil

1 cup chopped onion

1 cup diced red bell pepper

3 cloves garlic, minced

½ cup bottled salsa

½ cup lager beer (not dark)

1 can (14½ oz.) Mexican-style stewed tomatoes with jalapeño pieces

1 can (15 oz.) black beans, rinsed and drained

¼ cup (1 oz.) grated Monterey Jack or cheddar cheese

Minced fresh cilantro (optional)

---

DIABETIC EXCHANGE: ¾ STARCH   ¼ CARBOHYDRATE   2 VEGETABLE   2¼ FAT   3 VERY LEAN MEAT

CALORIES: **293**   FAT: **8 G**   SAT. FAT: **2 G**   CARBOHYDRATES: **27 G**   PROTEIN: **27 G**   CHOLESTEROL: **57 MG**   SODIUM: **823 MG**   FIBER: **6 G**

# Moroccan Chicken Stew with Lemon

1 Stir together the garlic, ½ cup of the scallions, lemon juice, cumin, and allspice in a large bowl. Add the chicken and toss until well coated. Cover with plastic wrap and refrigerate for 20 to 30 minutes.

2 Meanwhile, heat the oil until hot but not smoking in a flameproof casserole over medium heat. Add the squash and onion and cook, stirring frequently, until the squash and onion are lightly golden, about 5 minutes.

3 Stir in the chickpeas, broth, and parsley and bring to a boil. Add the chicken with its marinade, reduce to a simmer, cover, and cook until the vegetables are tender and the chicken is cooked through, about 8 minutes.

4 Combine the cornstarch and 1 tablespoon of water in a cup and stir to blend. Stir the olives, if desired, remaining ½ cup scallions, and the cornstarch mixture into the stew and boil, stirring constantly, until the stew is slightly thickened, about 1 minute. Spoon the stew into 4 bowls and serve.

**HEALTH NOTE** | *If you are looking for ways to minimize the amount of animal protein in your diet, this stew is a good choice. A small amount of chicken is paired with hearty protein- and fiber-rich chickpeas.*

**SERVES: 4**

4 cloves garlic, minced

1 cup sliced scallions

3 tbsp. fresh lemon juice

¾ tsp. ground cumin

⅛ tsp. ground allspice

¾ lb. skinless, boneless chicken breasts, cut into 2-inch chunks

1 tbsp. olive oil

2 cups peeled and seeded butternut squash, cut into 1½-inch chunks

1 medium red onion, diced

1 cup canned chickpeas, rinsed and drained

⅔ cup fat-free, low-sodium chicken broth

¼ cup chopped fresh parsley

2 tsp. cornstarch

¼ cup chopped pitted green olives (optional)

DIABETIC EXCHANGE: 1¼ STARCH   1 VEGETABLE   ¾ FAT   2¾ VERY LEAN MEAT

CALORIES: 248   FAT: 6 G   SAT. FAT: .8 G   CARBOHYDRATES: 25 G   PROTEIN: 25 G   CHOLESTEROL: 49 MG   SODIUM: 254 MG   FIBER: 5 G

# Turkey Tagine with Apricots and Honey

**SERVES: 4**

1 cup couscous

1 cup boiling water

¼ cup flour

2 tsp. paprika

1 tsp. ground coriander

¾ tsp. ground cumin

¼ tsp. salt

½ tsp. cinnamon

1 lb. turkey cutlets, cut crosswise
into 1-inch-wide strips

1 can (14½ oz.) fat-free,
reduced-sodium chicken broth

1 tbsp. olive oil

3 cups cubed butternut squash

1 cup diced turnip

½ cup dried Turkish apricots,
cut into pieces (see tip)

1 tbsp. white wine vinegar

1 Granny Smith apple, peeled,
cored, and cut into ¾-inch cubes

2 tbsp. dried currants

1 can (15 oz.) chickpeas,
rinsed and drained

1 Combine the couscous and boiling water in a medium heatproof bowl and let stand until the couscous is tender and the water is absorbed, about 5 minutes.

2 Combine the flour, paprika, coriander, cumin, salt, and cinnamon on a sheet of wax paper. Dredge the turkey in the flour mixture, shaking off and reserving the excess. In a small bowl, combine the reserved dredging mixture with the broth. Set aside.

3 Heat the oil until hot but not smoking in a flameproof casserole over medium heat. Add the turkey and cook until lightly browned, about 5 minutes. With a slotted spoon, transfer the turkey to a plate. Add the broth-flour mixture to the pan along with the squash, turnip, and apricots and bring to a boil, stirring occasionally, until the vegetables are firm-tender, about 10 minutes.

4 Return the turkey to the pan and add the vinegar, apple, currants, and chickpeas. Simmer until the turkey is cooked through and the apple is softened, about 5 minutes. Serve the turkey spooned over the couscous.

**TIP** *Dried Turkish apricots are whole rather than halved; they're plumper and less tart than California apricots. If you are using California apricots, soak them first in boiling water to cover for 20 minutes.*

DIABETIC EXCHANGE: 4¼ STARCH   ½ VEGETABLE   ½ FAT   3½ VERY LEAN MEAT

CALORIES: **568**    FAT: **7 G**    SAT. FAT: **.9 G**    CARBOHYDRATES: **86 G**

PROTEIN: **42 G**    CHOLESTEROL: **70 MG**    SODIUM: **618 MG**    FIBER: **9 G**

CURRANTS

APRICOTS

CINNAMON

# Spiced Chicken with Fennel

**SERVES: 4**

1 tsp. paprika

½ tsp. ground cumin

½ tsp. ground coriander

½ tsp. ground ginger

½ tsp. salt

¼ tsp. freshly ground
black pepper

4 skinless, boneless chicken
breast halves (1 lb. total)

1 tbsp. olive oil

2 cups thinly sliced fennel bulb
plus ¼ cup chopped fennel
fronds (see tip)

1 red onion, cut into 1-inch chunks

1 cup couscous

2 cups boiling water

¾ cup orange juice

⅓ cup fat-free, reduced-sodium
chicken broth

2 tsp. cornstarch mixed with
1 tbsp. water

1 Combine the paprika, cumin, coriander, ginger, ¼ teaspoon of the salt, and the pepper in a medium bowl. Add the chicken, turning to coat it well. Heat the oil in a large nonstick skillet over medium heat until hot but not smoking. Add the chicken and cook it until browned and just cooked through, about 5 minutes per side. Transfer the chicken to a plate.

2 Add the sliced fennel, onion, and ¼ teaspoon of the salt to the pan and stir-fry until the vegetables are crisp-tender, about 7 minutes.

3 Meanwhile, combine the couscous, the remaining ¼ teaspoon salt, and the boiling water in a medium bowl. Cover and let it stand until tender, about 5 minutes.

4 Add the orange juice and broth to the skillet and bring to a boil. Stir in the cornstarch mixture and boil, stirring, until slightly thickened, about 1 minute. Return the chicken to the pan along with the fennel fronds and cook until the chicken is just heated through, about 2 minutes. Serve with the couscous.

**TIP** | *To prepare fresh fennel, cut the stalks from the bulb, reserving the fronds. Trim the root end and any tough outer sections from the bulb, then slice it cross-wise. If you can't get fennel, substitute 2 cups of sliced celery and ¼ cup of chopped parsley; add ½ teaspoon fennel seeds to the other seasonings in Step 1.*

DIABETIC EXCHANGE: **2½** STARCH  **⅓** FRUIT  **2¼** VEGETABLE  **⅓** FAT  **4** VERY LEAN MEAT

CALORIES: **403**    FAT: **5 G**    SAT. FAT: **.9 G**    CARBOHYDRATES: **53 G**    PROTEIN: **35 G**    CHOLESTEROL: **66 MG**    SODIUM: **471 MG**    FIBER: **5 G**

1  In a food processor with a shredding blade, shred the apple, onion, and cabbage.

2  Combine the cornstarch, ¼ teaspoon of the salt, and ¼ teaspoon of the pepper on a plate. Coat the pork chops lightly with the seasoned cornstarch, transferring the excess cornstarch to a small bowl. Add the lemon juice to the bowl, stir, and reserve the mixture.

3  Heat the oil in a large nonstick skillet over medium-high heat until hot but not smoking and in it sauté the pork chops for 5 minutes on each side.

4  Add the apple juice concentrate and bring the liquid to a boil. Reduce the heat, cover, and simmer for 5 minutes. Transfer the pork chops to a plate and cover them loosely.

5  Add the shredded apple, onion, and cabbage to the skillet. Stir the reserved cornstarch mixture and add it to the skillet with the caraway seeds and the remaining salt and pepper. Simmer the mixture, stirring until thickened and the cabbage is tender, about 5 minutes.

6  Return the pork chops to the skillet and cook them 1 to 2 minutes, or until heated through. Serve each pork chop with some of the cabbage and apple mixture on top.

**SERVES: 4**

1 Granny Smith apple, peeled, cored, and quartered

1 small onion

¼ lb. green cabbage

2 tbsp. cornstarch

½ tsp. salt

½ tsp. black pepper

Four ¼-inch-thick, lean, boneless center-cut loin pork chops (1 lb. total)

1 tbsp. fresh lemon juice

1 tbsp. canola oil

½ cup frozen apple juice concentrate, thawed

½ tsp. caraway seeds, lightly crushed

**HEALTH NOTE** | *Cabbage is a cruciferous vegetable that may help to prevent some cancers; it is high in fiber, vitamin C, and potassium. Choose cabbages that are firm and heavy and free of yellowing leaves, splits, or soft spots.*

DIABETIC EXCHANGE: 1½ FRUIT   1 VEGETABLE   3¼ VERY LEAN MEAT

CALORIES: 301   FAT: 9 G   SAT. FAT: 2 G   CARBOHYDRATES: 27 G   PROTEIN: 26 G   CHOLESTEROL: 72 MG   SODIUM: 380 MG   FIBER: 2 G

GARLIC

PINEAPPLE

SOY SAUCE

1 Preheat the oven to 425°. Combine the pineapple juice concentrate, mustard, soy sauce, salt, and pepper in a small bowl.

2 Peel the garlic and cut each clove lengthwise into thirds. With a sharp knife, make 18 slits randomly in the pork loin. Tuck a piece of garlic into each slit.

3 Place the pork loin in a small roasting pan and brush it with half of the pineapple-mustard mixture. Add ½ cup of the broth and roast the pork loin for 30 minutes.

4 Meanwhile, quarter the potatoes and cut the carrots into ½-inch-thick slices. Spray a shallow pan with nonstick cooking spray, add the vegetables, and roast them until the pork is done.

5 Reduce the oven temperature to 350°. Brush the pork with the remaining pineapple-mustard mixture and continue roasting until it is cooked through and the internal temperature registers 160°, about 30 minutes more.

6 Remove the pork from the pan and let it rest for 5 minutes. Skim and discard the fat from the pan juices. Stir together the cornstarch and the remaining broth, and add to the roasting pan. Simmer over medium heat, stirring and scraping up the brown bits, for 2 to 3 minutes, or until the sauce is slightly thickened.

7 Slice the pork and serve it with the roasted vegetables and sauce.

**SERVES: 8**

⅓ cup frozen pineapple juice concentrate, thawed

3 tbsp. Dijon mustard

1 tsp. reduced-sodium soy sauce

¼ tsp. salt

¼ tsp. freshly ground black pepper

6 cloves garlic

1 small boneless pork loin (1¾ lb.)

1 cup fat-free, reduced-sodium chicken broth

1 lb. small red potatoes

3 medium carrots

2 tsp. cornstarch

**TIP** *Pork is much leaner today than it used to be, so be careful to not overcook it. Initially roasting at a higher temperature sears the roast's outside but keeps the meat tender and juicy inside.*

DIABETIC EXCHANGE: ⅔ STARCH   ⅓ FRUIT   ¾ VEGETABLE   2⅔ VERY LEAN MEAT

CALORIES: 251   FAT: 8 G   SAT. FAT: 3 G   CARBOHYDRATES: 20 G   PROTEIN: 24 G   CHOLESTEROL: 61 MG   SODIUM: 363 MG   FIBER: 2 G

**SERVES: 4**

2 tsp. canola oil

½ lb. mushrooms, wiped clean

½ lb. shallots, peeled

2 tbsp. honey

1 tsp. chopped fresh tarragon, or ½ tsp. dried tarragon

½ cup Madeira or port

2 tsp. cornstarch

½ cup fat-free, reduced-sodium chicken broth

¼ tsp. salt

Freshly ground black pepper

2 New York strip (or shell) steaks (about 10 oz. each), trimmed of fat and each cut into 2 pieces

1 Heat the oil in a nonstick skillet over medium heat; add the mushrooms and sauté them until they are lightly browned, about 4 minutes. With a slotted spoon, transfer the mushrooms to a bowl. Add 1 cup of water, the shallots, honey, and tarragon to the skillet. Bring the liquid to a simmer and cook the mixture until the shallots are translucent and only ¼ cup of liquid remains, 8 to 10 minutes. Stir in the mushrooms and keep the mixture warm.

2 Boil the Madeira or port in a small saucepan until reduced by half. Whisk together the cornstarch and 1 tablespoon of the broth. Stir the remaining broth and cornstarch mixture into the saucepan and simmer, stirring, for 2 minutes. Stir in ⅛ teaspoon of the salt and some pepper. Keep the sauce warm.

3 Preheat the grill or broiler.

4 Sprinkle the steaks with the remaining salt and pepper to taste, and grill or broil them for 3 minutes on each side for medium-rare meat. Serve the steaks with the glazed shallots and mushrooms on the side and topped with the sauce.

**EDITOR'S NOTE** | *Today's beef is generally leaner than it used to be but it can still add amounts of unwanted saturated fat to your meals. A handy rule of thumb: A 3-ounce cooked portion is about the same size as a deck of cards.*

DIABETIC EXCHANGE: **2** CARBOHYDRATE    **2** VEGETABLE    **3** LEAN MEAT

CALORIES: **292**    FAT: **10 G**    SAT. FAT: **3 G**    CARBOHYDRATES: **25 G**    PROTEIN: **26 G**    CHOLESTEROL: **62 MG**    SODIUM: **287 MG**    FIBER: **1 G**

GINGER

WATERCRESS

STEAK

1  Stir together the ginger, chili paste or pepper flakes, sherry, broth, corn-starch, and sugar in a bowl and add the beef. Marinate the beef, covered and refrigerated, for 1 hour.

2  Stir together the cucumbers, salt, vinegar, and sesame oil in a bowl. Refrigerate the salad.

3  Drain the beef, reserving the marinade. Heat the canola oil in a large, nonstick skillet or a well-seasoned wok over high heat. Add the beef and stir-fry it until well browned, about 2 minutes. Add the reserved marinade and stir constantly until the sauce thickens, about 1 minute. Add the watercress and toss the mixture quickly. Serve the stir-fried beef and watercress immediately, accompanied by the chilled cucumber salad.

**HEALTH NOTE** | *Watercress, which is high in beta carotene, vitamin C, and calcium but virtually calorie-free, is much more than a garnish. Choose crisp, tender leaves with uniform color. Store watercress in a plastic bag in the refrigerator and use the cress within a day or two. When looking for leaner cuts of beef, look for "loin" or "round" in the name.*

**SERVES: 4**

One 2-inch piece fresh ginger, peeled and minced

1 tbsp. chili paste, or 1 tsp. red pepper flakes

¼ cup dry sherry

¼ cup fat-free, reduced-sodium chicken broth

1 tbsp. cornstarch

1 tsp. sugar

1 lb. top round steak, trimmed of fat and sliced into 3-inch-long thin strips

2 cucumbers, seeded and cut into thick strips

¼ tsp. salt

¼ cup rice vinegar or distilled white vinegar

1 tsp. dark sesame oil

½ tbsp. canola oil

1 bunch watercress, trimmed, washed, and dried

DIABETIC EXCHANGE: ¼ CARBOHYDRATE    1 VEGETABLE    1 FAT    3½ VERY LEAN MEAT

CALORIES: 224    FAT: 7 G    SAT. FAT: 2 G    CARBOHYDRATES: 8 G    PROTEIN: 28 G    CHOLESTEROL: 65 MG    SODIUM: 263 MG    FIBER: 2 G

**SERVES: 6**

2 oranges

1½ lb. boneless sirloin steak, trimmed of fat and sliced into very thin strips

1 tsp. grated lemon zest

3 tbsp. cornstarch

2 tbsp. sugar

2 tbsp. canola oil

2 tsp. fresh ginger, cut into thin strips

¼ tsp. salt

⅛ tsp. cayenne

¼ cup rice vinegar or distilled white vinegar

1 lb. snow peas, stems and strings removed

**TIP** | *Use only the outermost skin layer of citrus fruit for zest, avoiding the bitter white pith. The aromatic oils in the zest are what adds so much flavor to foods.*

1  With a vegetable peeler, remove thin strips of peel from the oranges and slice them into shreds to make about ½ cup.

2  Squeeze the orange juice into a small saucepan; boil until reduced to about 3 tablespoons; set aside. Stir together the beef, lemon zest, cornstarch, and sugar in a large bowl; set aside.

3  Heat 1 tablespoon of oil in a large, nonstick skillet or a well-seasoned wok over high heat. Add the orange zest and ginger; cook, stirring constantly, for 1 minute; transfer to a plate; set aside.

4  Add one-third of the beef in a single layer to the hot skillet or wok and brown well—3 to 4 minutes—stirring frequently. With a slotted spoon, transfer the beef to the plate. Repeat this step twice with the remaining thirds of the beef, adding ½ tablespoon of the oil each time.

5  Once the third batch of beef is done, return the rest of the beef and the zest-ginger mixture to the skillet or wok. Add the salt, cayenne, vinegar, and orange juice; cook over high heat, stirring often, until the liquid evaporates—about 2 minutes.

6  While the beef is cooking, set a vegetable steamer in a saucepan, add 1 inch of water, and bring to a boil. Add the snow peas, cover tightly, and steam for 2 minutes. Transfer the snow peas to a warmed serving platter, mound the beef on top, and serve immediately.

DIABETIC EXCHANGE: ⅓ FRUIT   ½ CARBOHYDRATE   1¼ VEGETABLE   3½ VERY LEAN MEAT

CALORIES: **272**   FAT: **10 G**   SAT. FAT: **2 G**   CARBOHYDRATES: **19 G**   PROTEIN: **27 G**   CHOLESTEROL: **69 MG**   SODIUM: **165 MG**   FIBER: **2 G**

1 Preheat the oven to 500°.

2 Scatter the garlic cloves in a small baking dish and roast them until they are very soft—20 to 30 minutes. Let them cool.

3 Combine the juniper berries and peppercorns in a small bowl. Press the mixture into both sides of the steaks and set them aside at room temperature.

4 Combine the wine and the shallots or onion in a small saucepan, and boil the mixture until nearly all the liquid has evaporated, about 5 minutes. Add the broth and boil until it is reduced to about 1 cup, about 5 minutes.

5 Squeeze the garlic pulp from the skins into a food processor or a blender. Add the shallots with their liquid and puree until smooth. Put the garlic sauce (it will be thick) into the saucepan and keep it warm over low heat.

6 Preheat the grill or broiler.

7 Grill or broil the steaks for about 3 minutes on each side for medium-rare meat. Serve the steaks with the garlic sauce.

**SERVES: 4**

2 whole garlic bulbs, cloves separated but not peeled

½ tsp. crushed juniper berries

1 tsp. cracked peppercorns

4 lean beef tenderloin steaks (4 oz. each), trimmed of fat

1 cup red wine

3 shallots, sliced, or ½ small onion, finely chopped

2 cups fat-free, reduced-sodium chicken broth

**EDITOR'S NOTE** | *The juniper berries used in this special-occasion dish are astringent blue-black berries native to both Europe and America; you can find them in most gourmet groceries. They are generally crushed before use to release the pungent flavor. If they are unavailable, use 1 teaspoon gin for each 2 berries or use equal parts crushed bay leaves and caraway seeds.*

DIABETIC EXCHANGE: ¼ CARBOHYDRATE   1½ VEGETABLE   3 LEAN MEAT

CALORIES: 230   FAT: 9 G   SAT. FAT: 3 G   CARBOHYDRATES: 10 G   PROTEIN: 27 G   CHOLESTEROL: 71 MG   SODIUM: 372 MG   FIBER: .7 G

**MAKES 3 BOWLS**
**(14 one-cup servings)**

HERB FLAVORING

1 tbsp. unsalted butter

1 clove garlic, crushed

1 tbsp. chopped fresh mixed herbs,
   such as basil, parsley, and chervil

2 tsp. freshly grated
   Parmesan cheese

2 tbsp. pumpkin seeds

SPICE FLAVORING

1 tsp. dry mustard

1 tsp. tomato paste

½ tsp. hot red pepper sauce

1 tbsp. sesame seeds

CURRY FLAVORING

1 tsp. curry powder

1 tsp. turmeric

1 tsp. fresh lemon juice

1 tbsp. honey

1 tbsp. plain low-fat yogurt

2 tsp. canola oil

¾ cup popping corn

1   For the HERB FLAVORING: Melt the butter in a saucepan and add the garlic, mixed herbs, Parmesan, and pumpkin seeds. Cook, stirring, for 1 minute, then set the pan aside.

2   For the SPICE FLAVORING: Combine in another saucepan the mustard, tomato paste, and hot red pepper sauce. Bring the mixture to a boil, stirring, over medium-low heat; set aside.

3   For the CURRY FLAVORING: Combine in a third saucepan the curry powder, turmeric, lemon juice, and honey. Bring the mixture to a boil, stirring, over medium-low heat. Remove from the heat and stir in the yogurt.

4   While the flavorings are hot, pop the corn. Heat the oil in a large, heavy-bottomed saucepan, add the corn and cover with a lid. Heat over medium-low heat, shaking the pan, until all the corn has popped—2 to 3 minutes.

5   Pour approximately one-third of the popcorn into each of the flavorings and stir until evenly coated. When you stir the popcorn into the spice flavoring, add the sesame seeds. Serve warm in separate bowls.

**HERB FLAVORING:** DIABETIC EXCHANGE: ½ STARCH  ⅓ FAT

| CALORIES: 57 | FAT: 2 G | SAT. FAT: .7 G | CARBOHYDRATES: 8 G |
|---|---|---|---|
| PROTEIN: 2 G | CHOLESTEROL: 2 MG | SODIUM: 6 MG | FIBER: 0 G |

**SPICE FLAVORING:** DIABETIC EXCHANGE: ½ STARCH  ¼ FAT

| CALORIES: 50 | FAT: 2 G | SAT. FAT: .1 G | CARBOHYDRATES: 8 G |
|---|---|---|---|
| PROTEIN: 1 G | CHOLESTEROL: 0 MG | SODIUM: 8 MG | FIBER: .1 G |

**CURRY FLAVORING:** DIABETIC EXCHANGE: ½ STARCH  ⅛ CARBOHYDRATE  ¼ FAT

| CALORIES: 52 | FAT: 1 G | SAT. FAT: .1 G | CARBOHYDRATES: 9 G |
|---|---|---|---|
| PROTEIN: 1 G | CHOLESTEROL: .1 MG | SODIUM: 1 MG | FIBER: 0 G |

CAYENNE

LEMON

SESAME

1 Preheat the oven to 400°.

2 In a food processor, blend the shrimp, lemon juice, egg white, salt, sour cream, scallions, garlic, and cayenne until the mixture is minced.

3 Toast the bread until it is light brown. Remove the crusts and cut each slice into 4 triangles. Spread the shrimp topping over the toast and cover with an even sprinkling of the sesame seeds.

4 Place the triangles on the baking sheet and bake until they are golden brown—15 to 20 minutes.

**HEALTH NOTE** | *The classic version of this recipe is very high in fat. Baking the toasts instead of frying reduces fat content by more than half, while keeping lots of flavor.*

---

**MAKES 32 TOASTS**

12 oz. cooked, peeled, and deveined shrimp

2 tsp. fresh lemon juice

1 egg white

¼ tsp. salt

3 tbsp. low-fat sour cream

3 tbsp. finely chopped scallions

1 clove garlic, minced

¼ tsp. cayenne

8 thin slices white bread

2 tbsp. sesame seeds

---

DIABETIC EXCHANGE: ⅛ STARCH  ⅜ VERY LEAN MEAT

CALORIES: 25    FAT: .6 G    SAT. FAT: .1 G    CARBOHYDRATES: 2 G    PROTEIN: 3 G    CHOLESTEROL: 21 MG    SODIUM: 67 MG    FIBER: .1 G

**SERVES: 10**

1 red apple, cored and finely chopped

1 onion, finely chopped

1 cup fine dry breadcrumbs

½ cup dry champagne or other sparkling dry white wine

1 lb. ground turkey

¼ lb. pork loin, trimmed of fat and ground

½ tsp. salt

Freshly ground black pepper

1 Spray a nonstick skillet with nonstick cooking spray. Cook the apple and onion in the skillet, covered, over low heat until softened, about 4 minutes.

2 Combine the breadcrumbs, wine, turkey, pork, salt, some pepper, and the apple-onion mixture in a bowl, kneading with your hands to mix well.

3 Shape the sausage meat into 20 patties about ½ inch thick.

4 Heat a large, nonstick skillet over medium heat. Cook the patties in batches until they are browned and cooked through, about 2 minutes on each side. Serve the sausages at once.

**EDITOR'S NOTE** | *No need to delete sausages from your food plan. The apple lends a certain light sweetness, a perfect counterpoint to the savory turkey and pork.*

DIABETIC EXCHANGE: ½ STARCH    ⅛ FRUIT    ⅜ VEGETABLE    1½ LEAN MEAT

CALORIES: 157    FAT: 6 G    SAT. FAT: 2 G    CARBOHYDRATES: 11 G    PROTEIN: 12 G    CHOLESTEROL: 30 MG    SODIUM: 243 MG    FIBER: 1 G

1 Preheat the oven to 350°.

2 Scrub and dry the potatoes and slice them ¼ inch thick. Place half of the slices in a 1½-quart baking dish and sprinkle with half of the rosemary. Top the potatoes with half of the onions and spinach. Repeat the layers.

3 With a fork or whisk, beat together the milk, egg, and 3 tablespoons of the Parmesan and pour over the vegetables. Cover the dish with foil and bake for 50 minutes.

4 Remove the casserole from the oven and sprinkle it evenly with the remaining 1 tablespoon Parmesan and breadcrumbs. Bake the casserole, uncovered, another 10 minutes.

**SERVES: 4**

4 baking potatoes (2 lb.)

1½ tsp. dried rosemary, crushed

½ cup sliced onions

2 cups chopped fresh spinach leaves

1½ cups skim milk

1 egg

¼ cup grated Parmesan cheese

1 tbsp. dry breadcrumbs

**HEALTH NOTE** | *A hearty, healthy vegetarian dish that will remind you of a potato au gratin without all the cream and butter. Spinach also delivers many nutritional benefits; among other things, it is high in lutein, a phytochemical that may help keep your eyesight from failing.*

DIABETIC EXCHANGE: **3** STARCH ½ VEGETABLE ¼ HIGH-FAT MEAT

CALORIES: **263** FAT: **3 G** SAT. FAT: **2 G** CARBOHYDRATES: **47 G** PROTEIN: **13 G** CHOLESTEROL: **59 MG** SODIUM: **210 MG** FIBER: **5 G**

**SERVES: 6**

1 onion, sliced

Juice of 3 lemons

2-inch strip of lemon zest

8 parsley sprigs

3 fresh thyme sprigs, or
  ¼ tsp. dried thyme leaves

1 tsp. coriander seeds

½ tsp. cumin seeds

¼ tsp. salt

10 peppercorns

1 head of cauliflower, cut
  into florets

2 tbsp. olive oil

1 Combine the onion, lemon juice, zest, parsley, thyme, coriander, cumin, salt, and peppercorns in a deep, nonreactive skillet, with enough water to cover by 1 inch. Simmer the mixture for 10 minutes.

2 Raise the heat to medium high and add the cauliflower. Cook the florets, turning occasionally, until tender but not soft, about 10 minutes. Remove the pan from the heat and let the cauliflower cool to room temperature in the liquid.

3 Transfer the cauliflower to a vegetable dish with a slotted spoon and drizzle with the oil.

**HEALTH NOTE** | *Cauliflower, a cruciferous vegetable, is a great source of fiber. Crucifers, which include broccoli and Brussels sprouts, are thought to play a role in the prevention of some cancers. This marinade infuses the cauliflower with a tangy, lemon-herb flavor.*

DIABETIC EXCHANGE: 1¼ VEGETABLE    1 FAT

CALORIES: 67    FAT: 5 G    SAT. FAT: .6 G    CARBOHYDRATES: 6 G    PROTEIN: 1 G    CHOLESTEROL: 0 MG    SODIUM: 104 MG    FIBER: 2 G

THYME

CUMIN

CORIANDER

ORANGE ZEST

LIME

SHALLOTS

1 Whisk together the orange and lime juices, shallot, garlic, and zest. Whisk in the oil and vinegar and set aside.

2 Pour 1 inch of water into a large skillet and bring to a boil. Add the asparagus and cook until they are tender but still crisp, about 5 minutes. Drain and refresh them under cold running water, and refrigerate until you are ready to serve.

3 Arrange the asparagus on a large serving plate. Whisk the vinaigrette again and pour it over the asparagus.

**HEALTH NOTE** | *Asparagus provides good amounts of vitamins A and C for very few calories. Choose spears that are round, straight, and of uniform thickness with tight pointed tips that have not begun to flower. (If the asparagus is tender enough, you may choose not to peel it.) Be sure to cook only until the asparagus turn bright green; the color dulls when the spears are overcooked.*

**SERVES: 4**

1/3 cup fresh orange juice

1 tsp. fresh lime juice

1 tbsp. finely chopped shallot

1 tsp. finely chopped garlic

1 tbsp. slivered orange zest (avoid the white pith)

2 tbsp. extra virgin olive oil

1 tbsp. red wine vinegar

20 medium asparagus stalks, trimmed and peeled

DIABETIC EXCHANGE: 1¼ VEGETABLE  1½ FAT

CALORIES: 91  FAT: 7 G  SAT. FAT: 1 G  CARBOHYDRATES: 6 G  PROTEIN: 2 G  CHOLESTEROL: 0 MG  SODIUM: 2 MG  FIBER: 1 G

# Stir-Fried Green Beans with Soy Sauce

**SERVES: 4**

2 tbsp. reduced-sodium soy sauce

1½ tsp. finely chopped
   fresh ginger

1 clove garlic, finely chopped

1½ tbsp. toasted sesame oil

1 lb. fresh green beans, trimmed

1 tbsp. sesame seeds

1  Combine the soy sauce, ginger, and garlic in a small bowl and set aside.

2  Heat the oil in a wok or large skillet over medium-high heat. Add the soy mixture and the beans and stir-fry for 3 minutes. Cover and allow the beans to steam until just tender, about 2 minutes. Stir in the sesame seeds and serve immediately.

**TIP** | *Use this method of stir-frying for other vegetables like broccoli, peppers, carrots, and snow peas.*

DIABETIC EXCHANGE: 1¾ VEGETABLE   1¼ FAT

CALORIES: 95   FAT: 6 G   SAT. FAT: .9 G   CARBOHYDRATES: 9 G   PROTEIN: 3 G   CHOLESTEROL: 0 MG   SODIUM: 306 MG   FIBER: 2 G

**SERVES: 4**

1½ lb. spinach, washed, stems removed; do not dry the leaves

½ lb. white potatoes, peeled and cut into ½-inch cubes

½ tsp. salt

1 tbsp. canola oil

1 medium onion, chopped

1 clove garlic, finely chopped

1 tsp. sweet paprika

⅛ tsp. cayenne

Freshly ground black pepper to taste

2 tsp. red wine vinegar

1  Steam the wet spinach in batches in a large, covered pot over medium heat for 2 to 3 minutes, or until wilted. Chop the spinach coarsely and set it aside.

2  Put the potato cubes in a saucepan with enough water to cover them and ¼ teaspoon of the salt. Bring to a boil, lower heat, and cook until just tender—5 to 7 minutes.

3  In a large, nonstick skillet, heat the oil over medium-high heat. Add the potatoes, onion, and garlic and cook, stirring, for 5 minutes. Sprinkle in the paprika, cayenne, and black pepper. Add the spinach and cook, stirring, until the mixture is warmed through, about 1 minute. Stir in the vinegar and the remaining ¼ teaspoon of salt and serve immediately.

**HEALTH NOTE** *Adding fiber-packed spinach offsets the potatoes' destablizing effect on blood sugar.*

DIABETIC EXCHANGE: ½ STARCH   1¾ VEGETABLE   ¾ FAT

CALORIES: **111**   FAT: **4 G**   SAT. FAT: **.3 G**   CARBOHYDRATES: **16 G**   PROTEIN: **5 G**   CHOLESTEROL: **0 MG**   SODIUM: **391 MG**   FIBER: **5 G**

TARRAGON

APPLE

PARMESAN CHEESE

1 Toss together the zucchini, carrot, apple, onion, Parmesan, tarragon, salt, and pepper in a bowl.

2 Pour 1 inch of water into a large pot, set a vegetable steamer in the pot, and bring the water to a boil. Fill the squash halves with the vegetable mixture and arrange in the steamer. Cover the pot tightly and steam the squash until tender, about 20 minutes. Transfer the squash to a platter and serve.

**TIP** *If you wish, the squash can be baked. Preheat the oven to 400°, pour enough water into a baking dish to fill it about 1 inch deep. Set the filled squash halves in the dish, cover tightly with foil, and bake until tender, about 45 minutes.*

**SERVES: 4**

1 zucchini, grated

1 carrot, grated

1 small apple, peeled, cored, and finely chopped

1 small onion, finely chopped

¼ cup freshly grated Parmesan cheese

1 tbsp. finely chopped fresh tarragon, or 1 tsp. dried tarragon

⅛ tsp. salt

Freshly ground black pepper to taste

2 acorn squash, halved and seeded

DIABETIC EXCHANGE: 1⅓ STARCH ¼ FRUIT 1 VEGETABLE ¼ HIGH-FAT MEAT

CALORIES: **171** FAT: **2 G** SAT. FAT: **1 G** CARBOHYDRATES: **37 G** PROTEIN: **6 G** CHOLESTEROL: **5 MG** SODIUM: **203 MG** FIBER: **11 G**

**SERVES: 4**

1 oz. dried wild mushrooms
(porcini or shiitake)

1 tbsp. unsalted butter

1 cup orzo

1½ cups fat-free, reduced-sodium
chicken broth

1 clove garlic, finely chopped

1 tsp. fresh thyme, or ¼ tsp.
dried thyme leaves

¼ tsp. salt

Freshly ground black pepper

1 Pour 1 cup of hot water over the dried mushrooms and soak them until they are soft, about 20 minutes. Remove the mushrooms from their soaking liquid and slice them into thin strips. Strain the soaking liquid through a fine-meshed sieve and reserve ½ cup of it.

2 Melt the butter in a large saucepan over medium heat. Add the orzo and the mushrooms and cook the mixture for 5 minutes, stirring frequently.

3 Add the reserved mushroom liquid, ½ cup of the broth, the garlic, thyme, salt, and pepper. Cook, stirring constantly, until the orzo has absorbed most of the liquid—7 to 8 minutes. Reduce the heat to low, add another ½ cup of broth, and cook, stirring constantly, until the liquid is absorbed—3 to 4 minutes. Repeat this process with the final ½ cup of broth, cooking the mixture until the orzo is tender but still moist. Serve the dish immediately.

**EDITOR'S NOTE** | *This dish is reminiscent of the creamiest risotto but it is made with orzo instead of rice. Orzo is a pasta shaped like rice; as it absorbs liquid, it becomes much like risotto but takes half the time to prepare.*

DIABETIC EXCHANGE: **2 STARCH**   **1 VEGETABLE**   ½ FAT

CALORIES: **217**   FAT: **4 G**   SAT. FAT: **2 G**   CARBOHYDRATES: **36 G**   PROTEIN: **8 G**   CHOLESTEROL: **8 MG**   SODIUM: **379 MG**   FIBER: **3 G**

1  Preheat the oven to 350°.

2  Pour 1 inch of water into a large saucepan, set a vegetable steamer in the pan, and bring the water to a boil. Add the broccoli, cover, and steam until tender—5 to 8 minutes. Remove the steamer from the saucepan and refresh the broccoli under cold running water; drain it thoroughly.

3  Combine the broccoli and the milk in a food processor and pulse the motor until it is coarsely pureed. (Do not overprocess; the mixture should not be smooth.)

4  In a large bowl, whisk together the ricotta, egg, 1 tablespoon of Parmesan, the garlic, nutmeg, salt, and pepper. Stir in the broccoli mixture.

5  Spoon the broccoli mixture into an 8-inch-square baking dish and sprinkle it with the remaining 2 tablespoons of Parmesan. Bake the gratin until it is firm and lightly browned—35 to 40 minutes. Cut the gratin into 6 squares or diamonds, arrange them on a large plate, and serve at once.

---

**SERVES: 6**

1 lb. broccoli, the florets separated from the stems, the stems peeled and cut into ½-inch pieces

¼ cup low-fat (1%) milk

½ cup low-fat ricotta cheese

1 egg

3 tbsp. grated Parmesan cheese

2 cloves garlic, finely chopped

¼ tsp. grated nutmeg

½ tsp. salt

Freshly ground black pepper

---

**EDITOR'S NOTE** | *This dish is like a soufflé but is easier to make.*

DIABETIC EXCHANGE: ½ VEGETABLE    ¼ LOW-FAT MILK    ½ LEAN MEAT

CALORIES: 69    FAT: 3 G    SAT. FAT: 1 G    CARBOHYDRATES: 6 G    PROTEIN: 6 G    CHOLESTEROL: 43 MG    SODIUM: 292 MG    FIBER: 2 G

# DESSERTS

Frozen Raspberry Yogurt

**SERVES: 6**

2½ cups frozen raspberries, thawed

2 cups plain low-fat yogurt

½ cup sugar

¼ cup crème de cassis (optional)

1  Puree the raspberries in a food processor or a blender. With a rubber spatula, force the puree through a fine sieve set over a bowl and discard the seeds.

2  Combine the puree with the yogurt and sugar and freeze the mixture in an ice-cream maker according to the manufacturer's directions. Alternatively, freeze the mixture in a shallow metal cake pan until solid, about 6 hours. Break into chunks and, working in batches, blend in a food processor until smooth.

3  If desired, pass the crème de cassis separately so that each diner can pour a little over the yogurt.

**EDITOR'S NOTE** | *Crème de cassis is brandy distilled from black currants.*

DIABETIC EXCHANGE: ½ FRUIT    ⅓ LOW-FAT MILK

CALORIES: **140**    FAT: **2 G**    SAT. FAT: **1 G**    CARBOHYDRATES: **29 G**    PROTEIN: **4 G**    CHOLESTEROL: **5 MG**    SODIUM: **53 MG**    FIBER: **0 G**

1 Puree all but ½ cup of the blueberries in a food processor or a blender. If you are using frozen blueberries, puree them all; they do not make a suitable garnish.

2 Force the puree through a fine sieve set over a bowl and discard the solids remaining in the sieve. Add the sugar and lemon juice to the puree and stir until the sugar has dissolved.

3 Freeze the mixture in an ice-cream maker according to the manufacturer's directions. Alternatively, freeze the mixture in a shallow metal cake pan until solid, about 6 hours. Break into chunks, and, working in batches, blend in a food processor until smooth.

4 The sorbet is best when served within 24 hours. Just before serving, garnish the sorbet with the reserved fresh blueberries.

**SERVES: 6**

4½ cups fresh blueberries, picked over and rinsed, or 4 cups frozen unsweetened blueberries

1¼ cups sugar

1 tbsp. fresh lemon juice

**HEALTH NOTE** *Among fresh fruits, berries are a top source of fiber and contain high levels of vitamin C; blueberries are a standout when it comes to delivering antioxidants. If desired, you can substitute any berry you like; raspberries and strawberries make great sorbets.*

DIABETIC EXCHANGE: 1 FRUIT   2⅔ CARBOHYDRATE

CALORIES: 223   FAT: .4 G   SAT. FAT: 0 G   CARBOHYDRATES: 57 G   PROTEIN: .7 G   CHOLESTEROL: 0 MG   SODIUM: 7 MG   FIBER: 3 G

**MAKES 12 BARS**

1 tbsp. butter

1 tbsp. brown sugar

1 cup rolled oats

¼ tsp. ground cinnamon

½ cup whole-wheat flour

½ cup apple juice

½ tsp. vanilla extract

1 banana, mashed

¼ cup dried currants or raisins

1 Preheat the oven to 350°. Spray an 8-inch-square baking pan with cooking spray.

2 Cream together the butter and sugar in a medium bowl. Add the oats, cinnamon, and flour and stir until combined.

3 Mix the apple juice, vanilla, and ½ cup of warm water in a small bowl, add to the dry ingredients, and stir well. Stir in the banana and currants.

4 Spread the dough into the prepared baking pan, smoothing the top with a rubber spatula, and bake for about 1 hour, or until the top is golden. Remove from the oven and cool in the pan on a rack. Cut the cake into quarters, then cut each quarter into 3 bars.

**TIP** | *Very ripe bananas make the best bars and breads; you can save them in the freezer for several months, until you're ready to use them.*

DIABETIC EXCHANGE: **1** STARCH

CALORIES: **79**   FAT: **2 G**   SAT. FAT: **.7 G**   CARBOHYDRATES: **15 G**   PROTEIN: **2 G**   CHOLESTEROL: **3 MG**   SODIUM: **11 MG**   FIBER: **2 G**

VANILLA

BANANAS

CURRANTS

CINNAMON

VANILLA

OATS

# Crisp Oatmeal Cookies

1  Preheat the oven to 375°. Line a baking sheet with foil. Spray the foil with cooking spray.

2  Beat the eggs and egg white, cinnamon, vanilla, salt, baking powder, and sugar in a bowl until the mixture forms a ribbon when the beater is lifted, about 3 minutes. With a wooden spoon, stir in the oil and the oatmeal.

3  Drop rounded teaspoonfuls of the dough onto the baking sheet, leaving about 2 inches between the cookies.

4  Bake the cookies until they are golden brown—10 to 12 minutes. The cookies will puff up at first, then sink down—a sign that they have nearly finished cooking. Let the cookies cool to room temperature on the foil before attempting to remove them. Store the cookies in an airtight container.

**MAKES ABOUT 48 COOKIES**

2 eggs plus 1 egg white

1 tsp. ground cinnamon

1 tsp. vanilla extract

¼ tsp. salt

4 tsp. baking powder

1½ cups sugar

2 tbsp. canola oil

2½ cups quick-cooking oatmeal

**TIP** | *For a spicier cookie, add allspice, nutmeg, or ginger in addition to the cinnamon.*

DIABETIC EXCHANGE: ⅔ STARCH

CALORIES: **50**    FAT: **1 G**    SAT. FAT: **.1 G**    CARBOHYDRATES: **9 G**    PROTEIN: **1 G**    CHOLESTEROL: **9 MG**    SODIUM: **57 MG**    FIBER: **.4 G**

Strawberries with Lemon-Strawberry Sauce

**SERVES: 8**

2 eggs

¾ cup plus 2 tbsp. sugar

¼ cup cornstarch

Grated zest of 2 lemons

½ cup fresh lemon juice

6 cups strawberries,
   hulled and sliced in half

1 carambola, thinly sliced (optional)

1  Whisk together the eggs, sugar, cornstarch, lemon zest and juice, and ½ cup of water. Bring the mixture to a boil over medium heat, stirring constantly, for 2 minutes. Set the mixture aside to cool.

2  Puree 1 cup of the strawberries in a food processor or a blender and stir into the lemon mixture.

3  Spoon the lemon-strawberry sauce into 8 individual dishes. Carefully set the remaining strawberries in the sauce; garnish each serving, if you like, with carambola slices.

**EDITOR'S NOTE** | *Carambolas are also called star fruit because when cut crosswise they have a star shape; their flavor ranges from sweet to lightly tart. Carambolas do not require peeling—they can be eaten right out of hand. Choose fruit that has an even golden yellow color and use within a few days of purchase.*

DIABETIC EXCHANGE: ⅔ FRUIT   1¾ CARBOHYDRATE   ¼ MEDIUM-FAT MEAT

CALORIES:157   FAT:2 G   SAT. FAT:.4 G   CARBOHYDRATES:35 G   PROTEIN:2 G   CHOLESTEROL:35 MG   SODIUM:18 MG   FIBER:3 G

**SERVES: 6**

2 tbsp. thinly sliced orange zest
(outer rind from 1 to 2 oranges)

2-inch length of fresh ginger,
cut into ¼-inch-thick rounds

⅔ cup sugar

1 tart green apple, quartered, cored,
and cut into ½-inch pieces

2 ripe peaches or nectarines, halved,
pitted, and cut into ½-inch pieces

1 pear, cored and cut into
½-inch pieces

1½ cups blueberries, picked over

3 tbsp. fresh lemon juice

1 Combine 4 cups of water, the orange zest, ginger, and sugar in a large saucepan and bring the mixture to a boil. Reduce the heat and simmer the liquid until it is reduced to about 2 cups of syrup. Remove the ginger with a slotted spoon and discard it. Let the syrup cool.

2 Combine the cut fruit, blueberries, and lemon juice in a large bowl and toss well.

3 Toss the fruit gently with the syrup and refrigerate, covered, until thoroughly chilled, about 1 hour and 30 minutes.

**HEALTH NOTE** | *This fruit dessert is a nutrition champion, packed with fiber and nutrients. You can use the tasty ginger syrup, which can be made in advance if desired, over frozen yogurt or other desserts.*

DIABETIC EXCHANGE: **1¼ FRUIT   1½ CARBOHYDRATE**

CALORIES: **161**   FAT: **.4 G**   SAT. FAT: **0 G**   CARBOHYDRATES: **41 G**   PROTEIN: **.8 G**   CHOLESTEROL: **0 MG**   SODIUM: **3 MG**   FIBER: **3 G**

GINGER

NECTARINES

BERRIES

1 Combine the cranberry juice, sugar, lemon and orange zests, vanilla, cinnamon stick, and cloves in a medium saucepan, and simmer the mixture for 5 minutes.

2 Add the pear halves and simmer for 15 minutes more, turning occasionally. Remove the pan from the heat and discard the cinnamon stick and cloves.

3 Transfer the pear halves and poaching liquid to a bowl and cool to room temperature, basting the pears often with the liquid if they are not completely immersed.

4 Refrigerate the pears at least 30 minutes, or until well chilled. Serve the pear halves with the poaching liquid spooned on top.

**SERVES: 4**

2 cups unsweetened cranberry juice

2 tsp. sugar

2 tsp. grated lemon zest

1 tsp. grated orange zest

1 tsp. vanilla extract

1 cinnamon stick

4 whole cloves

2 large pears, peeled, halved, and cored

**HEALTH NOTE** | *Studies show that cranberry juice contains compounds that improve blood vessel health, inhibit blood clots, and help deter oxidation of artery-clogging LDL cholesterol.*

DIABETIC EXCHANGE: 1⅔ FRUIT

CALORIES: 97    FAT: .4 G    SAT. FAT: 0 G    CARBOHYDRATES: 24 G    PROTEIN: .4 G    CHOLESTEROL: 0 MG    SODIUM: 4 MG    FIBER: 3 G

# Blueberry Cobbler

**SERVES: 4**

2 cups fresh blueberries

3 tbsp. maple syrup

½ cup unbleached all-purpose flour

¾ tsp. baking powder

½ tsp. ground cinnamon

⅛ tsp. salt

1½ tbsp. butter, melted

1 tbsp. skim milk

1 tsp. grated lemon zest

1 Preheat the oven to 400°.

2 Wash, stem, and pick over the berries. Combine berries and maple syrup in a saucepan and cook over medium heat, stirring occasionally, for 5 minutes, or until the berries are very soft. Remove the pan from the heat and set aside.

3 Stir together the flour, baking powder, cinnamon, and salt in a medium bowl. Add the butter, milk, and lemon zest and stir just until a soft dough forms. Turn the dough onto a lightly floured surface and roll it out with a floured rolling pin to a 9-inch round.

4 Pour the berry mixture into a 9-inch pie plate and lay the dough on top. Bake the cobbler for 25 minutes. Let it cool 5 minutes before serving, cut into quarters, and serve warm.

**HEALTH NOTE** | *Unlike most cobblers, which have heavy crusts made with loads of butter or shortening, this one is topped with a satisfying yet light, lemon-flavored pastry.*

DIABETIC EXCHANGE: ¾ STARCH    ⅔ FRUIT    ⅔ CARBOHYDRATE    ¾ FAT

CALORIES: **177**    FAT: **5 G**    SAT. FAT: **3 G**    CARBOHYDRATES: **33 G**    PROTEIN: **2 G**    CHOLESTEROL: **12 MG**    SODIUM: **217 MG**    FIBER: **2 G**

# Pear Bread Pudding

1 Preheat the oven to 375°. Arrange four 8-ounce custard cups on a baking sheet.

2 Peel and core the pears and cut them into ½-inch cubes. Whisk together the eggs and milk in a small bowl.

3 Stir together the flour and sugar in a bowl; gradually whisk in the milk mixture in a stream. Stir in the lemon zest and almond extract.

4 Divide the pears and bread cubes among the custard cups. Pour the custard over the bread and pears (it will not completely cover them) and stir gently to coat.

5 Bake the pudding for 25 to 30 minutes, or until the custard is set and golden brown on top. Serve the bread pudding hot or at room temperature.

**SERVES: 4**

2 ripe pears (1 lb. total), or 4 juice-packed, canned pear halves, drained

2 large eggs

1 cup skim milk

2 tbsp. unbleached, all-purpose flour

2 tbsp. sugar

1 tsp. grated lemon zest

1 tsp. almond extract

4 slices day-old whole-wheat bread, cut into ½-inch cubes

**TIP** | *Make sure the bread is at least one day old. The older the bread, the more the pudding will retain its shape. If you do not have day-old bread, then cube the bread as directed and toast the cubes in a single layer on a baking sheet in a 350° oven until lightly browned.*

DIABETIC EXCHANGE: 1¾ STARCH    1 FRUIT    ½ MEDIUM-FAT MEAT

CALORIES: 232    FAT: 4 G    SAT. FAT: 1 G    CARBOHYDRATES: 41 G    PROTEIN: 9 G    CHOLESTEROL: 107 MG    SODIUM: 213 MG    FIBER: 5 G

HONEY

BROWN SUGAR

CURRANTS